I0818253

ONE BILLION STARTS WITH ONE

HOW TO SHARE JESUS WITHOUT BEING RELIGIOUS

TIM DILENA

Carpenter's Son Publishing

Published by Carpenter's Son Publishing
Carpentersonpublishing.com

Cover and Interior Design by HybridStudios.com

Printed in the United States of America

ISBN: 978-1-968127-25-1 (print)

ONE BILLION STARTS WITH ONE

HOW TO SHARE JESUS WITHOUT BEING RELIGIOUS

TIM DILENA

To all the front line ministries and ministers who still go to the city streets, the remote villages, and university campuses. To those who go into closed nations and still preach from street corners. To those unnamed and unashamed who proclaim the gospel every day. You are an inspiration and you are not forgotten.

Thank you for being the one.

CONTENTS

INTRODUCTION

This book was birthed in a midtown Manhattan restaurant by a pastor's statement and request. This was the first time I had lunch with Pastor Andy and his church is 3,500 miles from New York City. He pastors in London, England. He told me that he watches Times Square Church services each week and is encouraged. Then he challenged me. These words came like a wrecking ball. He said "Pastor Tim, shepherds don't make sheep but sheep make sheep. The church needs to be equipped in soul winning." I was challenged and convicted. Andy was right.

Times Square Church has a mission and a mandate to win one billion souls to Christ. To read these words without faith will neither inspire nor excite. We have a passion to go beyond our city, our nation, and into the nations. Times Square Church ministers to over 130 countries every week from New York City. Through technology and in person, we extend our reach to almost every nation around the world sharing the gospel. But technology is not enough; it's just a tool. To be truly effective, there must be multiplication, not addition, or a billion souls is just a fantasy. Addition usually happens from one person who is passionately trying their hardest to influence others with that same excitement they have. Addition is locally real but globally ineffective. To reach the world, there must be multiplication. Multiplication is when people are equipped, not just excited. One billion starts with one really is the way toward multiplication and winning the world to Christ. The second "one" is you.

This project is to equip the "one" in the body of Christ for the Great Commission. It is to challenge us to be soul winners. Soul winners is a lost phrase in the church today. It is also to remind us that there is a Jesus challenge called "THE GREAT COMMISSION." While churches are stuck on their vision, many have forgotten that we have already been given the vision by Jesus. Many don't know what the "GREAT COMMISSION" is because many have not heard that there is a Great Commission. Matthew 28 is the Great Commission when Jesus said in verses 19–20 (NKJV): 19 "Go therefore and make disciples of all the nations, baptizing them in the name of the Father and of the Son and of the Holy Spirit, 20 teaching them to observe all things that I have commanded you; and lo, I am with you always, even to the end of the age." What is sad is that it's possible to live out the Christian life without doing the things that Jesus commanded us to do. We have hired people and support people to share the gospel, feed the hungry, visit the prisons, clothe the naked, and care for widows and orphans. Money and support are effective, but they are not meant to remove responsibility. The average church member doesn't have to concern themselves with these Great Commission items because they are being done for them. Hudson Taylor, the great missionary who brought the gospel to China, said, "The Great Commission is not an option to be considered; it is a command to be obeyed."[1] Being a soul winner is not a professional job for a few trained men, but instead it is the commission and responsibility of all those who call themselves a follower of Christ. One of my spiritual fathers, Leonard Ravenhill, believed for the church to be awakened to obedience. He once said, "Isn't it staggering when you think that one sermon on the day of Pentecost produced 3,000 people? And we have a city where 3,000 sermons are preached today and nobody was saved. And it doesn't even faze us."[2]

I am hoping *One Billion Starts with One* fazes us. I am praying it moves us to saying, "I'll be the one." I'll be the one in my home, job, university, city, nation and around the world. We need sheep to produce sheep. I hope those words do to you what it did to me. Charles Spurgeon didn't hold anything back when he spoke to his congregation in the nineteenth century these words: "Have you no wish for others to be saved? Then you are not saved yourself, be sure of that."[3] Say that today and people will leave the church, stop giving, post that it's condemning and find a more comfortable place on Sundays. When we feel our hearts are pricked or pierced as it says in the book of Acts, these are Holy Spirit conviction words. I believe as you go through these chapters you will feel that piercing. I challenge you to bring these chapters to your church, your small group, your ministry and let's be part of a Master Vision called the Great Commission. Mother Teresa once said, "We are all pencils in the hand of a writing God, who is sending love letters to the world."[4]

God, make me a pencil to tell the world that You love them. Let me be the one.

BE SURE YOUR SIN WILL FIND YOU OUT

I once read about a police officer from a Midwestern state who pulled a driver over and asked for his license and registration. The driver asked, “What's wrong, Officer? I didn’t run any red lights. I certainly wasn't speeding.”

“No, you weren't,” said the officer, “but I saw you waving your fist as you swerved around the lady driving in the left lane, and I further observed your flushed and angry face as you shouted at the driver who cut you off. Then you pounded your steering wheel when the traffic came to a stop near the bridge.”

The man asked, “Well, is that a crime, Officer?”

“No, but when I saw that ‘Jesus loves you’ bumper sticker on the car, I figured the car was stolen!”

The man was living a contradiction. It was a “word and life” contradiction.

When the Apostle Paul wrote to a young pastor named Titus, he wasted no time warning him about this word and life contradiction. Paul said in Titus 1:16, “They say they know God but their actions speak louder than their words” (MSG).

Paul was reminding Titus that you can be speaking to people without your mouth even moving. As they say, actions speak louder than words. People outside of the church aren't so much listening to our words as they are watching our lives. Brennan Manning, an author from whom I've gained valuable insight, wrote these words: "The greatest single cause of atheism in the world today is Christians who acknowledge Jesus with their lips, walk out the door, and deny Him by their lifestyle. That is what an unbelieving world simply finds unbelievable."[5] We see it happen all the time—whether during a sports award ceremony or the Grammy Awards. Many stars thank God with their lips, but what later comes out of their mouth and permeates their lifestyle denies Him to those around them. Jesus said, "These people make a big show of saying the right thing, but their heart isn't in it" (Matthew 15:8 MSG).

People will follow your footsteps much more quickly than your words or advice. The right words without the right life will inevitably send the wrong message. As we look toward one billion souls, I want to start by challenging our Sunday church attendance, our claps, and our shouts to God. I want to make sure it is all backed up during the rest of the week by how we behave. We want to get rid of the word and life contradiction.

I grew up in the church and was raised by two godly parents, for whom I am very thankful. But I do remember growing up with verses that would be used against us kids. For instance, I knew that Deuteronomy 21:21 spoke of stoning the children for rebellion. And then there was Revelation 21:8 which said all liars go to hell. I would even get some extrabiblical things thrown at me. "You don't go to the movies because what if Jesus comes back at that moment?" I never understood that one. I just figured that when they built theaters, they made the ceilings rapture-proof so nobody would be able to leave to go to heaven. However, one of the scariest verses that was pointed at me is found in the book of Numbers.

Let me tell you a story before I get to the verse. My father, the son of an Italian immigrant, worked his way up from a beat cop in the New York City Police Department to eventually become one of the chiefs of the New York City Transit Department before the departments merged. To be part of an Italian Pentecostal family was such a great blessing, but when it came to correction, I wish my dad knew about this thing that they do today called timeout. We never had that in our household. We started with the wooden spoon. Then as we got older, we graduated to the belt.

I was born in the early sixties, a time when silver coins were still in circulation. There were silver quarters, silver half dollars, and sometimes even silver dollars. Whenever my dad stopped at a store, he would collect any silver coins he received as change and put them in a bag. A father collecting silver coins and a young son with a deep desire for baseball cards turned out to be a foolproof formula for creating a thief. I would sneak into my dad's room while he was sleeping and take money to go buy baseball cards in Long Island . . . until one day when my mom saw me come out of the room with my pockets jingling.

"Where did you get that money?" she demanded.

"Jesus blessed me," I explained.

Of course, she knew I wasn't that spiritual. I still remember the moment. We were up on the second floor of our Long Island house when she warned me, "If you don't tell me the truth, I'm going to pray, and God is going to tell me!" And then came the words that would forever echo in my mind: "Be sure your sin will find you out!"

Well, that's all it took. With my mom about to pray and now this verse stuck in my mind, all I could say was, "I'm a thief! I'm a liar! Here it is. It's Dad's money!"

This is the verse I want to talk about. Moses was speaking in Numbers 32:23: “But if you will not do so, behold, you have sinned against the Lord, and be sure your sin will find you out” (NASB).

In business school, the professors often say: “Cash is king.” Biblical hermeneutics, or the study and interpretation of the Bible, has a king as well. Context is king. Bible interpretation can get inflated because people fail to read what comes before and after a passage. Reading passages in context helps us understand why those words were used and what they refer to. We need to learn to read the whole Bible, not just verses.

“Be sure your sin will find you out” had nothing to do with stealing money to buy baseball cards. The verse is not saying that if you are secretly living in sin, it will be exposed. There are plenty of other verses that deal with that, but not this verse. So what does this verse actually mean? What is the story behind it? What is the sin that will find you out?

The context of this verse concerns a promise that two tribes of Israel made to fight for their brothers. After the Children of Israel wandered in the wilderness for 40 years, a new generation was ready to go in and fight for the Promised Land. But when they reached the edge of the Promised Land at a city called Gilead, two tribes, Gad and Reuben, suddenly said, “We don't want to go in. We want to build homes on the nonbattle side of the Jordan. We'd rather stay here than fight over there” (see Numbers 32:1–5).

Understandably upset, Moses then spoke these words to the sons of Gad and the sons of Reuben: “Shall your brothers go to war while you yourselves sit here?” (Numbers 32:6 NASB)

His concern was that they would go into Canaan and be down two tribes when fighting for the Promised Land. It was as if Gad and Reuben would stop at the edge, build their homes and in a sense think, “Hey, I got my stuff together. My house is built, my second house is now down south, therefore I'm done with the fight. Good luck to all of you folks! I'll watch online and let you fight the rest of the battle.” Here was Moses's response to them:

> Now why are you discouraging the sons of Israel from crossing over into the land which the Lord has given them? This is what your fathers did when I sent them from Kadesh-barnea to see the land. (Numbers 32:7–8 NASB)

Moses was likening such a decision to the ten spies who brought back a bad report, ultimately discouraging the rest of the Israelites and resulting in 40 years of wandering. If they choose now to stay in Gilead, it will discourage the others from going in.

Gad and Reuben insisted that even if they build their homes on this side of the Jordan, they would remain committed to fighting for the other tribes to attain their possession. “We will not return to our homes until every one of the sons of Israel has possessed his inheritance” (Numbers 32:18 NASB). In other words, if you let us build here, we will fight with you; we will fight for our brothers and sisters. Moses responded:

> If you will do this, if you will arm yourselves before the Lord for the war, and all of you armed men cross over the Jordan before the Lord until He has driven His enemies out from before Him, and the land is subdued before the Lord, then afterward you shall return and be free of obligation toward the Lord and toward Israel, and this land shall be yours for a possession before the Lord. (Numbers 32:20–22 NASB)

Then Moses continued on to the verse we are looking at:

> But if you will not do so, behold, you have sinned

> against the Lord, and be sure your sin will find you out. (Numbers 32:23 NASB)

This is not the verse we should use when sending our kids out on a Friday night: "Okay, you can go out with your friends, but be sure your sin will find you out!" There are other ways to scare them. It is we who should be scared of this verse. This verse should make us very sober, for the sin here is so subtle. Moses was essentially saying, "If you settle because you now have your life together, and you break this agreement to fight for your brothers, that is a sin, and that sin will find you out."

What does this story mean for us? It is a commitment to refuse to sit while others are going to war. Perhaps God has blessed your business. God has blessed your athletic ability or your acting ability. God has blessed your career, whatever it may be. God would remind us, "Now that you've attained a certain status in life, don't forget you still have to fight for other people. Just because you won your battle doesn't mean the war is over. This is bigger than you think." You are not done when you get what you want. You were called not only to your own victory but to help others attain theirs.

We have a phrase that we often use at church. Our leaders, elders, and sometimes even our staff will use it. When we are in a difficult situation, we'll encourage each other with these words: "This is why we fight." It means that our battles have purpose. We are fighting for others.

Ezra's testimony is a perfect example of this. Ezra was baptized a few months ago, and this is his story as he wrote it:

> I was a transgender person until a year ago when I was saved by Jesus. My story is that I transitioned into the lifestyle of a woman since I was 18 years old. Since I was 6 years old, I was always into feminine things and was

always attracted to men. I have lived with my partner for 18 years and been married for 9 years. Besides being happily content, and at the time I considered myself blessed for being in love. Through the ups, I was also dealing with insecurities. I started having severe anxieties to the point where I would fear just leaving our apartment to get our mail. I was scared of other people's judgment to the point it was traumatizing just to leave the house. I realized this lifestyle opened you to spiritual attacks. I noticed it was even spreading to my family members. They started having problems at work and fights with each other at home. Like we were being attacked by tormenting spirits. I felt tortured mentally and emotionally. Our minds were constantly stressed and negative. It got to the point where I felt very hopeless.

After hearing a gospel song on YouTube, it gave me a sense of peace. A friend at the time confronted the demonic spirit inside of me, where I had no idea these things were real. I felt the demon respond through me, and from there it opened my eyes to the truth that God is real, spirits are real, and heaven and hell are real. Because of that, I was able to surrender to Jesus and declare Him as Lord over my life and mean it. At that moment, He showed me a vision of Him descending from heaven's gates; He was anointing me in the spirit. Around that same night, I felt the enemy of God in my room. I felt him choke me, saying, “This one is mine.” I realized because he had put so much work and effort into me and my family, there was a spiritual battle going on over my soul. I remember saying, “I choose Jesus,” and I felt him back away as Jesus appeared. At that time, I was still in sin. God had to open my spiritual eyes to show me He was with me and fighting for me.

> The attacks escalated to the point where God had to lead me to repentance and close doors. He gently and slowly led me away from my ex-partner, and we eventually got divorced. It was a hard process, but knowing full well what was at stake, I wanted myself and my loved ones to be saved.
>
> Normally, this would not have been possible, but through God's grace, we were able to have peace and acceptance through the process. Even giving up on female estrogen pills was a challenge because my body was reliant on these for two decades. I was very hormonal because my flesh and spirit were in battle.
>
> I couldn't accept the reality of things, but I chose to just trust in Jesus and His love. I eventually changed my name, cut my hair and changed my clothes to what is acceptable to Him. The lesson is to surrender to Jesus and let Him lead you into repentance. Because on our own it will be almost impossible. It's through Him that the impossible was achieved. My priority is to chase eternal life with Jesus even if I have to leave everything behind. I still get tempted and attacked, but God shows me He is with me, He strengthens me, and provides for me and my family. He gave me hope. Thank you, Lord Jesus!!! I love you with all my heart and soul!!!

This is why we fight! We fight so Ezra can know Christ and have a changed life. We don't sit down and say, “I got my business, I got my 401k. I got what I want, so I'm done fighting, praying, and giving. I will just have a seat now.” No, we cannot stop fighting. The sin is when it becomes all about your world. That's the sin that Moses was talking about. Moses was concerned that Gad and Reuben were getting so caught in their own world that they were losing sight of the bigger cause. You and I have an assignment: We are called to fight for others. There are people who need to be born again and changed by the power of Jesus Christ. We must remain committed to the Great Commission around the world. We must make a commitment not to sit while others go to war.

We know why we fight; we fight for other people. Now let's take a moment to look at ways we fight for others.

We fight by praying for people.

My wife Cindy and I have a list of prodigals that we pray for every night. The list is constantly growing as we encounter more parents with wayward children. The greatest joy we have is when we get to take somebody off that list because he or she came back to Jesus. But it's a fight. You fight when you pray for people, bringing them before the Lord by name.

We fight by serving people.

Whether you are ushering at your church, working in the nursery, playing an instrument, singing in the choir, moving knobs on a soundboard, cleaning the sanctuary—you are serving people. Every time we serve, we are fighting for people to be born again. Every person who serves is a soldier in the fight to bring someone back to the Lord.

We fight by giving.

We fight when we give in order that the gospel may go forth. Recently our Bible school, Summit International School of Ministry, was at Yale University leading worship among hundreds of students. Because of the financial generosity of our congregation, we were able to send the entire student body to Yale and also have our general overseer, Pastor Carter Conlon, preach the gospel right in the middle of the campus and see students come to Christ. There was a young man from China who heard the gospel there. He got saved and immediately felt an urgency to bring the Good News back to his nation. This is why we fight!

We fight by being concerned enough to ask people about eternity.

How do we broach the topic of eternity with people? How do we enter into these types of conversations with people? I will be discussing this in the chapters ahead so that you will feel equipped to share the gospel with others.

Let me now take you to a terrifying scene that Jesus describes for us—one that is important for us to consider in light of the verses we looked at in Numbers. It takes place at the end of time:

> When the Son of Man appears in his majestic glory, with all his angels by his side, he will take his seat on his throne of splendor, and all the nations will be gathered together before him. And like a shepherd who separates the sheep from the goats, he will separate all the people. The 'sheep' he will put on his right side and the 'goats' on his left. Then the King will turn to those on his right and say, "You have a special place in my Father's heart. Come and experience the full inheritance of the kingdom realm that has been destined for you from before the foundation of the world! For when you saw me hungry, you fed me. When you found me thirsty, you gave me something to drink. When I had no place to stay, you invited me in, and when I was poorly clothed, you covered me. When I was sick, you tenderly cared for me, and when I was in prison you visited me."
>
> Then the godly will answer him, "Lord, when did we see you hungry or thirsty and give you food and something to drink? When did we see you with no place to stay and

> invite you in? When did we see you poorly clothed and cover you? When did we see you sick and tenderly care for you, or in prison and visit you?"
>
> And the King will answer them, "Don't you know? When you cared for one of the least important of these my little ones, my true brothers and sisters, you demonstrated love for me."
>
> Then to those on his left the King will say, "Leave me! For you are under the curse of eternal fire that has been destined for the devil and all his demons. For when you saw me hungry, you refused to give me food, and when you saw me thirsty, you refused to give me something to drink. I had no place to stay, and you refused to take me in as your guest. When you saw me poorly clothed, you closed your hearts and would not cover me. When you saw that I was sick, you didn't lift a finger to help me, and when I was imprisoned, you never came to visit me."
>
> And then those on his left will say, "Lord, when did we see you hungry or thirsty and not give you food and something to drink? When did we see you homeless, or poorly clothed? When did we see you sick and not help you, or in prison and not visit you?"
>
> Then he will answer them, "Don't you know? When you refused to help one of the least important among these my little ones, my true brothers and sisters, you refused to help and honor me." And they will depart from his presence and go into eternal punishment. But the godly and beloved 'sheep' will enter into eternal bliss. (Matthew 25:31–46 TPT)

Here is what C. S. Lewis said regarding this passage: "The heaviest charge against each of us turns not upon the things he has done but on the things he has never done, perhaps never dreamed of doing."[6] In other words, they were condemned not because of what they did but because of what they failed to do. It was the sin of omission. It was the sin of sitting and doing nothing.

Am I saying that if we don't help the poor that we are going to go to hell? No, that is not what I'm saying, and that is not what Jesus is saying. We are saved by grace, not works. Just because you help the poor, it doesn't mean that you are saved. On the other hand, if you're not helping the poor, it doesn't mean that you are not saved. However, when the love of Jesus truly gets inside of you, you want to fight for others.

Sometimes when I travel to a city and I get there a little bit early, I will find a used bookstore. I always ask for the Christian or the religious section. It's never very big. Over the years, most of my best treasures were found on the bottom shelf, probably because nobody wants to get down that low. It's amazing what treasures you can find when you kneel down!

I once came across a book containing the last 18 speeches that Mother Teresa spoke around the world before she died. I picked up the book, read one story and then concluded that I needed to have this book. Here is the story that I read in the bookstore that day:

> I remember very vividly some time ago visiting a magnificent nursing home for the elderly. It had everything you could ever want. There were 40 patients there. They had every need met. But one strange thing happened . . . everyone sat and looked at the door. I did not see a single person with a smile on their face. I turned to the worker on duty and asked her, "Sister, why is it that these people, who have everything here, keep looking toward the door?"

> "It happens every day. They are waiting and hoping for a son or daughter (or anybody) to come and visit them. They are hurt because they are forgotten. They always say, 'Maybe today someone from my family will come and visit me.'"[7]

"Maybe today someone from my family will come." But no one ever came. That was the context of Numbers 32. We'd better make sure our brothers are not staring at the door, waiting for us, yet we never show up! I don't want anyone to say, "They never came. They never talked to me about salvation. They never prayed with me." I don't want to just sit in the church and sing. I want to be the one who opens the door—who shows up to fight for people's lives.

Jesus said it this way in the book of Matthew:

> Be generous with your lives by opening up to others because you'll prompt people to open up with God, this generous Father in heaven. (Matthew 5:16 MSG)

Have you heard the old story about a mythical church attended only by ducks? The story is widely attributed, though perhaps erroneously, to Søren Kierkegaard, a nineteenth-century Danish philosopher and theologian, and goes like this:

> One Sunday morning all the ducks came into the church, waddled down the aisle and into their pews, and squatted. Then the duck minister took his place behind the pulpit, opened the duck bible, and read, "Ducks! You have wings, and with wings you can fly like eagles. You can soar into the sky! Use your wings!" All the ducks yelled "Amen!" and they all waddled home.
>
> This goes on in the lives of Christians to this very day, when faced with the truths and challenges of God to be like

> Jesus. They say "wonderful," "amen," "what a challenge from God," and then they waddle home.[8]

I challenge you not to waddle but to fly. God has given us victory in many areas of our lives. I believe He is saying to us today, "You got the victory. Now it's time to fight so somebody else can get the victory too." It is time to move into action, to be part of an army that is set on winning a billion souls. Don't miss the opportunity by saying "amen" to this chapter and then waddling away.

02

I'M NOT ASHAMED, I'M JUST SCARED

There is a well-known hymn we sing in church and also shirts we wear during water baptisms that feature its lyrics: "I Have Decided to Follow Jesus." I have even seen these words on shirts worn in different places across the country. However, few are aware that four people gave their lives so we could have those lyrics—a family who was unashamed of the gospel of Jesus Christ. Here is the incredible story of this hymn's origins, dating back more than a century ago in India:

> About 150 years ago, there was a great revival in Wales. As a result of this, many missionaries came to north-east India to spread the Gospel. The region known as Assam was comprised of hundreds of tribes who were primitive and aggressive headhunters. Into these hostile and aggressive communities came a group of missionaries from the American Baptist Missions spreading the message of love, peace, and hope in Jesus Christ. Naturally, they were not welcomed.
>
> One missionary succeeded in converting a man, his wife, and two children. This man's faith proved contagious and many villagers began to accept Christianity.
>
> Angry, the village chief summoned all the villagers. He

then called the family who had first converted to renounce their faith in public or face execution. Moved by the Holy Spirit, the man said: "I have decided to follow Jesus."

Enraged at the refusal of the man, the chief ordered his archers to arrow down the two children. As both boys lay twitching on the floor, the chief asked, "Will you deny your faith? You have lost both your children. You will lose your wife too."

But the man replied: "Though no one joins me, still I will follow."

The chief was beside himself with fury and ordered his wife to be arrowed down. In a moment she joined her two children in death. Now he asked for the last time, "I will give you one more opportunity to deny your faith and live."

In the face of death the man said the final memorable lines: "The cross before me, the world behind me. No turning back."

He was shot dead like the rest of his family.

But with their deaths, a miracle took place. The chief who had ordered the killings was moved by the faith of the man. He wondered, "Why should this man, his wife and two children die for a Man who lived in a far-away land on another continent some 2,000 years ago? There must be some remarkable power behind the family's faith, and I too want to taste that faith." In a spontaneous confession of faith, he declared, "I too belong to Jesus Christ!" When the crowd heard this from the mouth of their chief, the whole village accepted Christ as their Lord and Savior.

The song is based on the last words of Nokseng, a man

> from Garo tribe of Assam India. It is today the song of the Garo people.[9]
>
> This hymn continues to be sung all around the world 150 years later. Even today it is sung by the Garo people as a reminder that the words were originally spoken by one of their own—an unashamed believer willing to die for his faith.

Similarly, in the book of Romans, the Apostle Paul declared:

> For I am not ashamed of the gospel of Christ, for it is the power of God to salvation for everyone who believes, for the Jew first and also for the Greek. (Romans 1:16 NASB)

However, I believe something has happened in the church today where our cry has instead become, "I'm not ashamed of the gospel, I'm just a little apprehensive to share it." For this reason, over the next few chapters, I hope to equip the church to confidently share the gospel. I can't help but wonder if there are groups of people that have not gotten saved or songs that have not been written simply because we have become apprehensive about sharing the message that would change the world. The Garo tribe was converted because of Nokseng's courage and faith. Times Square Church and Teen Challenge exist because a skinny Pennsylvania pastor was unashamed to go to the worst gangs in the worst parts of Brooklyn, New York, to share the gospel. An unashamed man, David Wilkerson led Nicky Cruz to saving faith. Our world today needs the unashamed church once again.

I understand why many Christians might be apprehensive about sharing the gospel in today's volatile culture. Evangelism is tough in an increasingly uncivil and even litigious society. Healthy conversations rarely exist and are often replaced with personal attacks, insults, and rage directed toward those who are trying to win souls. As a result, the church fearfully waits for someone, like the Philippian jailor, to pointedly ask, "What must I do to be saved?" (See Acts 16:30.) At that point, we will suddenly be unashamed to share the gospel. But as for cold calls and street evangelism, we leave that to the borderline "crazy" Christians.

I was coming home the other day on the NYC subway, and as soon as the doors shut, a woman started to proclaim, "I was in trouble, I was lost. I was going to hell, I was depressed, but Jesus changed me! I'm a miracle, and He can change you!" Suddenly the subway doors opened in Times Square, and she walked out of the train. She was a miracle because while most of us will sit back and judge her as being a little "off," we fail to recognize that we are probably the ones who need to be judged. We have become an apprehensive, timid church. What happened to us? What removed the courage and boldness from the church today?

I do not present this as an accusation, but rather as my perspective after pondering and praying about the issue: I believe one of the key factors contributing to our apprehension came in the '90s when the seeker-friendly church emerged, which still exists today. The evangelistic voice was taken from the congregation and put on a stage. We told the church, "You invite them to church, and we'll take care of the rest. We'll make the music, create the right environment with smoke and lights, wear certain kinds of clothing like T-shirts with a suit, and our message will be friendly—winning them to Christ." As a result, we have silenced the church's evangelistic voice. No one in the pew feels the burden to share the gospel any longer. The task of soul winning has been taken away from the people in the church, leaving them soul-winning illiterate. Some of us don't even know how to start a conversation with the lost for fear that if it goes beyond a few sentences, we won't know what to say.

That is the danger of seeker-friendly churches. We've asked you to invite people but not become lifesavers yourself. The modern-day church has equipped its people to be nothing more than a mailman with an invitation to a Saturday or a Sunday service. But we are called to be more. We are called to be soul-winners, unashamed of this gospel.

Recent statistics show that almost one-third of all Muslim conversions to Christ start with a Jesus dream or Jesus vision. I have personally met individuals who have come to faith this way. Some years ago, I met a Muslim woman who became a believer, and I even had the privilege of baptizing her in our church in Detroit. The Lord had appeared to her in a dream when she was living in Iran. When she came to the United States to attend the University of Detroit, she noticed someone in her class that "looked different." She pulled that classmate aside and asked her what the dream meant. That classmate happened to be our worship leader, who then sent the Muslim woman to me. We met in my office and she told me, "Jesus has appeared to me and told me that He has risen from the dead. What am I supposed to do now?" Since Jesus was personally evangelizing to this Muslim woman, I certainly did not want to mess it up! I said, "Do what Jesus tells you to do!" She became an unashamed believer. As she was being baptized, I remember her standing in cold water and saying over a microphone, "I want to go back to my country and share this message, even if it means I will die!"

I've heard testimonies at our church where individuals had a similar experience—a vision or a dream of Jesus brought them to faith. Oftentimes the dream or vision somehow pointed them to somebody else to actually lead them to Christ. I don't want believers feeling unequipped or apprehensive to stop any of those moments. That is why it is so critical that we become the unashamed church once again.

As we look to the Scriptures, we see God challenging us to be unashamed in two specific locations:

> So he was reasoning in the synagogue with the Jews and the God-fearing Gentiles, and in the market place every day with those who happened to be present. (Acts 17:17 NASB)

To be unashamed in the synagogue and in the marketplace—that's our challenge today. Some people struggle to be bold inside the church. They find it difficult to lift their hands high in praise or to openly declare Jesus is Lord. If we can't do it in church, how can we expect to do it in public, the marketplace?

Even if we have learned over the past few decades to be bold in church, how can we be unashamed in the marketplace as well? Out in the marketplace is where one billion starts with one. To desire to be unashamed is to desire to be a soul-winner, and the Bible tells us that "he who is wise wins souls" (Proverbs 11:30 NASB). What happens to those who are wise like this? It says in Daniel 12:3 that "those who are wise shall shine like the brightness of the firmament, and those who turn many to righteousness like the stars forever and ever" (NKJV). I like how it reads in The Message translation:

> Men and women who have lived wisely and well will shine brilliantly, like the cloudless, star-strewn night skies. And those who put others on the right path to life will glow like stars forever. (Daniel 12:3 MSG)

Those wise people who win souls—they glow! I believe that's what the Muslim woman at the University of Detroit saw in her classmate when she noticed something different about her. Have you ever had someone notice that about you?

I was reading the biography of one of the greatest evangelists in America, Charles Finney, who pastored a church in New York City in the early nineteenth century. His church met at the Chatham Garden Theater in lower Manhattan. According to his biography, Charles Finney would not let anyone preach from his pulpit who wasn't a soul-winner, for he considered them to be unwise. He said, "Those are the best educated ministers, who win the most souls."[10]

So what exactly is a soul-winner? The book of James gives us one of the greatest definitions:

> My dear brothers and sisters, if someone among you wanders away from the truth and is brought back, you can be sure that whoever brings the sinner back from wandering will save that person from death and bring about the forgiveness of many sins. (James 5:19–20 NLT)

Soul winning is bringing people back to life by bringing them to Jesus. At the close of his life, David Brainerd, the great eighteenth-century missionary, wrote in his diary: "I cared not how I live nor what hardships I went through if I only might gain souls for Christ."[11] Of course, being a soul-winner in today's society will require great courage. It is a call for the unashamed.

If the thought of soul winning makes you apprehensive, how can you overcome that? Let me share with you my journey, as I remember coming to the end of myself one day. I was tired of being nervous about evangelizing, tired of not liking it, and tired of seeing no fruit. It was when I was 19 years old, and David Wilkerson asked me to spend the summer in Detroit, Michigan. They put us on the streets of Detroit with a stack of tracts—little gospel booklets—in our hands. We were sent out at noon, Monday through Friday, and were instructed not to return until 5 p.m. For five hours a day, 25 hours a week, this 19-year-old kid who was coming straight from Baylor University in Waco, Texas, walked the streets of Detroit, completely at a loss for what to do. It wasn't explicitly told to us, but we knew we should not come back with tracts. And I have to be honest, there were a few times when I hid the tracts in an abandoned building so they would think I handed them all out!

I wanted to be a soul-winner, but I was scared to death. I simply didn't know what to do or say. One day I got desperate and told God, "I've been out there for 25 hours a week. We've been doing this for three months, and nobody has come to Jesus. I am the worst soul-winner in the nation, maybe the world. All those hours and nobody has gotten saved." And all of a sudden, I remember telling God this: "I'm going to wake up an hour earlier than usual, and I'm going to pray for that hour. I'm going to pray that You do something and save somebody!" That's how my prayer life was birthed. It started because I was sick of failing. I was tired of nobody getting saved, and I didn't know what to do other than to ask God.

The first weeks and even months of trying to pray for an hour was a challenge, especially for someone who really didn't pray that much. I would get in about a good three minutes of prayer before 57 minutes of mind wandering. There were no cell phones to serve as a distraction back then, so the only thing I could do was sit there. But that is how I started every morning. "Lord, give me somebody to get saved." I'll never forget what came out of that. Not only was my prayer life birthed, but God began to work in my heart. And to this day, whenever I hear the word "Tennessee"—whether referring to the state or in some other capacity, it brings joy to my heart. Tennessee was my breakthrough in soul winning.

It wasn't a place; it was the nickname of a 50-year-old alcoholic. He'd been drinking on the streets of Detroit for 30 years. He came from Nashville, Tennessee, and I found him sitting on the stairs in front of an abandoned building. I shared the gospel for the first time with him, and his heart was wide open. I began to think maybe I had been praying for him one of those mornings. I put a track in his hand and wrote my number down, telling him that if he was really honest and serious, he could call me. I'll never forget getting a call from him that night around 2 a.m. He called and said, "I'm in downtown Detroit. Ever since you told me about this Jesus and the Holy Ghost, I've been hearing voices. I'm ready to get saved!" I drove downtown, picked that man up, and took him to Teen Challenge. I watched Tennessee go through Teen Challenge, get a job, live a life for Jesus, and join me in that triple X theater that we turned into a church. I watched Jesus do His work in Tennessee's life up until the day I officiated at his funeral.

The following is not meant for condemnation but simply to encourage you to pause and reflect: When was the last time you led someone to Christ? Or have you ever led somebody to Christ? If the Bible says that those who win souls are wise, we want to start there. I do not intend this to be a call to repentance if you haven't won someone to Jesus. Rather, I want to equip you by giving you what I call "the path to unashamed." My goal is to help us become the unashamed church once again. Drawing upon my own journey, here are three things that I believe will help you become a soul-winner.

1. DON'T "GO" UNTIL YOU "COME."

Time with Jesus and sharing the good news are inseparable. Prayer is the voice of faith. People ask me, "If I'm not ashamed of the gospel, why is it so hard to tell other people?" I believe that the reason often has to do with lack of prayer. We would be wise to yield to Jesus's two commands:

> Come to Me, all you who labor and are heavy laden, and I will give you rest. (Matthew 11:28 NKJV)

and

> And Jesus came and spoke to them, saying, "All authority has been given to Me in heaven and on earth. Go therefore

> and make disciples of all the nations, baptizing them in the name of the Father and of the Son and of the Holy Spirit, teaching them to observe all things that I have commanded you; and lo, I am with you always, even to the end of the age." (Matthew 28:18–20 NKJV)

Come into the presence of Jesus, then go into all the world and share the gospel. In Matthew chapter 9, Jesus calls those who are supposed to be witnessing "laborers" (see verses 37–38). He invites them to come to Him, and then He later commands them go into all the world and share the gospel. It also says this in the book of Mark:

> And He appointed twelve, so that they would be with Him and that He could send them out to preach. (Mark 3:14 NASB)

This is what Jesus Himself taught His disciples—the very ones who, as it says in Acts, would turn the world upside down (see Acts 17:6). This was His plan: "Before you go, come. Come be with Me so that you might be able to go out and do this."

I remember working with a young lady on our staff who had a powerful prayer life. God began to speak to her and lead her to minister in grocery stores. Sometimes He would tell her to go to the store and buy milk, and then He would give her a word for someone. One time she said God told her to go to the 10 items or less checkout line. As she was checking out, she looked at the cashier and said, "Thank you for doing this. You've been having a hard time with your marriage."

The cashier scanned her items, admitting, "Yes."

She continued, "You don't think God loves you. But God sent me here today to tell you that He loves you." In literally three minutes or less, she was telling the cashier what she received from the presence of Jesus, giving her hope again!

Come before you go. Spend time in His presence, and God will open up the door. I encourage you to think of one person you want to be born again and commit to praying for him or her every day for a year. Even if it is just a quick whisper on your way to work, "God, save them today." As you begin to pray, watch and see what God will do—which leads to our next step.

2. STAY ALERT FOR OPEN DOORS.

Here is the Apostle Paul's exhortation to us:

> Pray diligently. Stay alert, with your eyes wide open in gratitude. Don't forget to pray for us, that God will open doors for telling the mystery of Christ, even while I'm locked up in this jail. Pray that every time I open my mouth I'll be able to make Christ plain as day to them. Use your heads as you live and work among outsiders. Don't miss a trick. Make the most of every opportunity. (Colossians 4:2–5 MSG)

Paul's desire was not simply to preach from a pulpit. He wanted God to open doors when he was in jail and every time he opened his mouth! Open doors are God-appointed opportunities, so Paul is reminding us to pray for those moments. As you pray for that particular person every day, be prepared for when God opens up a door. But be aware that with each opportunity, there will undoubtedly be a battle that comes with it. The devil will not easily release people from going to hell. He will fight against it, and he will start with you. The attacks will be nervousness, uncertainty as to whether this is an open door, lack of faith, fear, apprehension—everything to try to stop you from opening up your mouth. Yet the Apostle Paul told a young pastor named Timothy to be ready to preach at all times:

> Proclaim the Word of God and stand upon it no matter what! Rise to the occasion and preach when it is convenient and when it is not. Preach in the full expression of the Holy Spirit—with wisdom and patience as you instruct and teach the people. (2 Timothy 4:2 TPT)

I am married today because I'm a soul-winner. I was unashamed about sharing the gospel with Cindy when I first met her. At the time, our church had been meeting in this triple X theater without any air conditioning. I would sweat every time I wore a tie. Cindy, vice president of the bank, along with the president of the branch, came to our church one day because we were interested in taking out a loan. After Cindy asked for our financials, I said to her, "Hey, before you go, can I just tell you that God loves you and that He has a plan for your life?" I started to share with her what it means to be born again. I then gave her a book called *More Than a Carpenter* by Josh McDowell. Cindy went home that night, read the book, said the prayer at the end, and showed up at church the next day. She was eventually baptized, filled with the Holy Ghost, and now she is my wife!

So come to Jesus and begin to pray for people. Pray for an open door, and then look out for it. And finally . . .

3. DON'T GO TO BATTLE WITHOUT YOUR SWORD.

When the door opens, don't go to battle without your sword. The book of Hebrews says:

> For the word of God is alive and powerful. It is sharper than the sharpest two-edged sword, cutting between soul and spirit. (Hebrews 4:12 NLT)

A paraphrased version says it like this:

> His powerful Word is sharp as a surgeon's scalpel, cutting

> through everything, whether doubt or defense, laying us open to listen and obey. Nothing and no one can resist God's Word. We can't get away from it—no matter what. (Hebrews 4:12–13 MSG)

When we are sharing with people, it is important to remember that Satan works through lies. The only thing that fights the power of satanic lies is the power of God's Word. When people object, "Well, I was raised in a different religion. I don't know about this Jesus stuff. What about the crusades? What about all the pastors who have fallen into sin?" the Word of God will cut through all of that, breaking down every lie.

As you are talking to someone about Christ, have the Bible ready—even if it is on your phone. The Word of God will work in the soul before you see it on their face. That's why you can't be upset, concluding that nothing is happening. Someone may fight you on the outside because there is an internal battle going on as the Word works deeply inside their heart.

Charles Spurgeon put it this way: "The Word of God is like a lion. You don't have to defend a lion. All you have to do is let the lion loose. The lion will defend itself."[12] The lion will start going after people's lives, just as He did in Thomas's story:

> I was born and raised in the southern part of Germany, and even though I went through the traditional Catholic rituals (baptism as a baby, communion, and confirmation), I never had a connection to the Christian faith, let alone a relationship with Christ. I went through life on the notion that I had to achieve everything myself.
>
> I finished school at the age of 16, started an apprenticeship at a bank in Munich, and worked myself up the corporate ladder. When I was 24 years old, my company offered me

a two-year assignment in New York. I did not hesitate to sign the contract. I arrived in New York on October 31st, 2001, and I spent the next couple of years enjoying the city as much as I could. I did not think about God; I did not miss God. I was fine. From time to time, I would visit this church on Broadway with colleagues and friends—Times Square Church. Not for worship, but for listening to gospel music. Usually, we snuck out once the choir stopped singing, but sometimes we would stay and listen to what the preacher had to say. Sometimes we were impressed by the sermon, but most of the time, we didn't really care.

But then, a couple of things happened that changed my life. One day, I got a new colleague, and she would turn out to really get on my nerves. She would talk a lot about this Jesus guy, and how my life was wrong. She kept talking about sin and everlasting life, and I really didn't want to hear it anymore. To my surprise, the very next Monday, she gifted me a NIV Study Bible, and said "You know, I want you to understand what you read. Then we can debate." I was shocked. Why would she do that?

Anyways, I followed her advice and started reading the book of John. I actually took the Bible on a vacation to Barbados, and while sipping on a glass of rum, I thought to myself: "What if this is the truth?" And as I read through the pages, studying the commentary, and thinking about the storyline, I came to the conclusion that her faith was ok. And that is what I told her. I said "Let's have peace. I understand now where you are coming from, and I'll respect it." But for her, that was not enough.

The financial crisis came, I got married, and fast forward to 2008. My wife, from Kenya, and I decided to hike up Mount Kilimanjaro. On the day before we left, my colleague told me that I needed to find a church. "You are not growing," she said, but you "need to grow, you need to accept Christ." I brushed her off and said that I was fine, and that I surely don't need any more growth. Boy, was I wrong.

As we were hiking up that mountain, I was pondering thoughts about God. And at one point, I asked God: "God, if You really exist, why don't You show yourself to me?" And He did show Himself right then and there. It was the first time that I heard God speak in an audible voice to me, and all He said was, "Thomas, I have a way for you." I didn't know what was happening, but one thing I knew: I needed to find a church. And fast. When I came down from that mountain, I was a different person, but I wasn't quite there yet.

Upon our return, I told my colleague about what had happened, and I started looking for a church. I tried a number of churches, and they were all full of nice people. But something was missing. They all had nice tea sessions after service, and good talks, but something was not there. Then I remembered this church on Broadway, and one Tuesday evening, I visited Times Square Church again. Remember, I had no understanding of the Holy Spirit yet, but when I walked through the doors that evening, I knew that I had found my church. The something I missed in all the other churches was right here. That evening, I heard about New Believers classes, and I signed up the next Friday. My wife even joined me for my class, and after the first class, she told me that I would end up as a teacher here. I laughed. Anyways, one Friday I asked one of my teachers if we could meet up to discuss some questions.

> We agreed to meet after next Sunday's service. During this service, my thoughts were just on one thing: "God, what is that way You have for me?" I can't remember the sermon. But I remember that the pastor said, "If this is you, then come to the altar and give your life to Jesus." I didn't think twice. I followed the altar call and just said this little prayer: "God, who am I kidding. You told me that You have a way for me, and I want to walk it with You. I have no idea what I am signing up for, but I want to walk with You." That was it. On March 1st, 2009, I got saved, and in September of that same year, I got baptized. And yes, I ended up as a teacher in the New Believers class of TSC.

God has been so faithful all these years. God is not done with me yet, He has a way for me, and I intend to walk it. To Jesus be the glory. Amen.

Thank God that Thomas's colleague was unashamed and boldly shared the gospel with him! What do you think would happen if each one of us became soul-winners in the spheres of influence where God has placed us? Each of us plays a crucial part in the vision to win a billion souls. Let's start by storming heaven for that one person, and then stay alert for open doors. Be ready in season and out of season. Let the Word of God—the lion—out of the cage to do its work in the soul!

03

TALKING TO MEN IN DRESSES

I had a conversation some time ago that changed me unlike any other encounter I've had with the unsaved. What I learned from the exchange became a foundational part of how I share the gospel, and it has continued to help me win souls over the years. It happened when I was talking to two men in dresses.

Less than 24 hours before that conversation, I was sharing the gospel with an entirely different group of people—the New York Yankees. Donnie, a friend of mine who is now with the Lord, was one of the most effective professional sports chaplains I've ever known. He was the chaplain of the Oakland A's baseball team for decades. He led MLB players, front office staff, and even umpires to Christ. After leading them to the Lord, he would pray for them to be filled with the Holy Ghost. He was unashamed of the gospel.

I would go out to California occasionally to help Donnie with the youth camps he ran, and during some of those visits, he would ask me to speak at the MLB chapel for the visiting team that was playing that day. We would meet in the players' weight room between batting practice and often have only 17 minutes to talk about Jesus.

One Sunday afternoon, the visiting team was the New York Yankees, and Donnie asked if I would do the chapel for them. I remember saying these words to the players in the weight room, all dressed in the pinstripes of the most iconic uniform in the world: "This evening I'm going to catch a red-eye flight from Oakland Airport to speak to the people at our church's soup kitchen in Detroit, Michigan. I want you to understand this: I will preach the same message to the hungry and the homeless that I just spoke to you in this stadium. It's the same message because, regardless of who you are—whether you're in pinstripes or you're homeless—our hearts are all the same."

This holds true for all of us today. Whether your clothes cost $5 or $5,000, whether you put on an NFL uniform, scrubs, or something that you got from the Salvation Army, our hearts all need Jesus Christ.

Less than 24 hours after speaking to men in pinstripes, I ended up speaking to two men in dresses. After preaching and serving food at our soup kitchen, I would always sit down at the tables with the people we served, eager to hear their stories. That day I sat down with two transvestites who called themselves Tracy and Toya—and had a conversation that forever changed the way I witness to people. I hope to equip you for soul winning with what I learned that day.

After proper introductions between us, the two men didn't hold anything back, posing this question to me: "Reverend, will we go to heaven looking like this?"

I was shocked. I didn't know how to respond, so I asked them this: "What do you think?"

Toya responded, "No way."

Tracy said, "Judge not, lest you be judged."

Toya then said, "This really concerns me. I really need to know."

Here is what I told them: "Let's hear what God has to say because

God always tells the truth. We hear what God has to say every time we open up the Scriptures." It is always a good idea to use the Bible. Let the Bible be the centerpiece of everything we do.

But before turning to the Scriptures, I started a journey with this statement: "If I tell you the rules without you knowing the Father who made the rules, then the commands He gives, the laws He pronounces over our lives, will seem abusive and controlling. You have to know who the Father is first." That's the problem with religion. Religion gives you the rules without the relationship. We tell people a lot about the rules but not enough about the Father.

Tracy and Toya expected me to read something from Leviticus or Deuteronomy. There is a verse in Deuteronomy that I did not read. It says, "A woman shall not wear man's clothing, nor shall a man put on a woman's clothing; for whoever does these things is an abomination to the Lord your God" (Deuteronomy 22:5 NASB). They expected me to go straight to the rules, but that is not what I did that day.

I then asked Toya, "If you see any of my children crying because of a house rule we enacted and you didn't know me, you could easily pass judgment upon me. Without understanding why we put a rule in place, you might conclude that I make my children miserable. That's because you don't know me or the sacrifices I've made for my kids. You are judging me based on a rule, not on who I actually am. When I say something that disagrees with my children's will, for example, 'You can't eat Oreos for breakfast,' they start crying. They may disagree, and their obedience may come with complaints and tears. But there is something they will always know. What is it, Toya?"

"That you love them and want the best for them," he replied.

"Exactly. When you see the crying, the pain, and the complaining, don't judge me just yet, unless you know who I am. That's where we need to get you both so that when you get your answers from God, you will know that He loves you—even when He disagrees with your lifestyle. The second thing is that if God's answer does disagree with you, what will you do? Who is right then? Will you choose what you want or what God wants?" I looked at Toya and asked, "Have you ever been wrong?"

"Yes."

"So have I. Do you think God has ever been wrong?"

Tracy said, "No."

I continued, "Then let's see what the Word has to say." Instead of giving them verses on sexual orientation and lifestyle from Deuteronomy and Leviticus, I did something they didn't expect. I gave them a passage on the character of God.

When it comes to rules, let's consider the most well-known rules the world has ever heard: the Ten Commandments. These universal laws have been displayed in public places, on government buildings and in justice halls. Here are the Ten Commandments that God gave to Moses:

> You shall have no other gods before Me. You shall not make for yourself an idol, or any likeness of what is in heaven above or on the earth beneath or in the water under the earth. You shall not worship them or serve them; for I, the Lord your God, am a jealous God, visiting the iniquity of the fathers on the children, on the third and the fourth generations of those who hate Me, but showing lovingkindness to thousands, to those who love Me and keep My commandments. You shall not take the name of the Lord your God in vain, for the Lord will not leave

> him unpunished who takes His name in vain. Remember the sabbath day, to keep it holy. Six days you shall labor and do all your work, but the seventh day is a sabbath of the Lord your God; in it you shall not do any work, you or your son or your daughter, your male or your female servant or your cattle or your sojourner who stays with you. For in six days the Lord made the heavens and the earth, the sea and all that is in them, and rested on the seventh day; therefore the Lord blessed the sabbath day and made it holy. Honor your father and your mother, that your days may be prolonged in the land which the Lord your God gives you. You shall not murder. You shall not commit adultery. You shall not steal. You shall not bear false witness against your neighbor. You shall not covet your neighbor's house; you shall not covet your neighbor's wife or his male servant or his female servant or his ox or his donkey or anything that belongs to your neighbor. (Exodus 20:3–17 NASB)

Here are all the rules, but who is the Father behind these rules? Who is the God that has given these rules? The problem arises when we jump right to verse three and forget what God said just prior. "Let me tell you something about the Father who wrote these rules," I said to the two men sitting before me. And then I read them this verse:

> I am the Lord your God, who brought you out of the land of Egypt, out of the house of slavery. (Exodus 20:2 NASB)

This verse is epic. Before God gives the Ten Commandments, He tells His people who He is and what He has done for them! God was saying to His people, "Let me tell you about how I set you free, delivered you, and broke your chains of bondage—before I tell you what to do!"

To skip verse 2 makes God confusing and turns Christianity into a religion. I've seen famous Christian leaders on national TV fumble the ball when asked questions regarding the rules. I've seen it happen on *The Oprah Winfrey Show*, *Larry King Live* and the *Today Show* when they were asked questions like: "What do you think about same-sex relationships? Are other religions going to heaven or only Christians? What about abortion?" They were being set up, and they all missed it. I don't say that critically, but the problem was that they were trying to address the rules without talking about who the Father is. When I get asked about the rules, my response is always this: "Can I share with you about who God is first before I tell you what He expects?" That's Exodus 20:2. You cannot know God from what He demands. You must know who He is and what He has done for you.

As you and I are an active part of what God is doing in this billion-soul harvest, we are going to be asked difficult questions. So when somebody asks you about an issue that society accepts but the Bible warns against, for instance, "What does God think about me smoking weed? What does God think about porn? Can I be a man and wear a dress?" you can respond, "If you're only giving me a few minutes, then I can't answer your question. But if you give me 20 minutes to discuss who God is first, then the answer will make sense."

We must understand how critical this is. We have been taught to just stand firm and fight for what is right, failing to understand that people reject God's laws because they don't know who God is. When we leave out who God is and what Jesus has done, then none of it makes sense. Think about when your children come out of the womb. On the day they are born, do you start by giving them all the rules? "No spitting up. I'm not changing your diaper." Of course not! You kiss them and love them, and the rules are understood later. That is why we must tell people what God says in Exodus 20:2. This verse gives purpose to the greatest rules given to humanity.

Some years ago, I would get my hair cut by a girl who we will call Valerie. She was interested in God, even though she was living a lifestyle completely contrary to His Word. Before I left that city to move to New York, she became a Christian. I asked her, "I've been sitting in your chair for all these years. How did you get born again?"

She replied, "You sat in my chair and never told me how bad I was, but you told me how good God is. I gave my heart to Him, and I have no desire to live that kind of lifestyle anymore." Valerie allowed Exodus 20:2 sink in.

Let me share with you another story where a young woman was forever changed when she discovered the heart of the Father, not merely all the rules. This is Amy's story:

> Being from an Indian family, I was taught to get educated, have a career, marry the right man, start a family, and live a comfortable life with success and wealth.
>
> My plan to have this life started coming together when I met the man of my dreams at the age of 17, just after graduating high school. He was 21 then, a senior at NYU, heading off to med school. He became everything for me, my priority in every way. What I was too naive to recognize then was that he controlled me, and I submitted to his every whim and request. I didn't know any better. Culturally, I had been taught to submit, so I thought I was expected to do everything he asked me to do, even if it made me feel uncomfortable. This relationship lasted for 7 years, and just when I had finished grad school and started my career, and we were making plans toward marriage, he came to me and said that although he wanted to marry me, he wanted to "see what else was out there" before doing so.

That's when the life I had built collapsed right in front of me—everything I worked so hard to gain. I reached the lowest point of my life; utterly broken, depressed, filled with despair, guilt, and shame. I felt like a complete failure!

I had some basic understanding that God should be helping me through this, but going to the Orthodox church and obediently repeating the same thing every Sunday wasn't helping the situation. It wasn't helping me come out of the despair, guilt, and shame I was feeling.

That's when I remembered that there was this church my sister and her friends used to go to while she was in college: Times Square Church. I had gone to the church twice when I was at NYU doing grad school. I didn't really understand everything that was happening, but something was different. There was something so peaceful about it, something joyful even. It reminded me a little bit of the Sunday School I used to go to in my old neighborhood.

So, in early 2002 I started coming to Times Square Church on Tuesday nights week after week. For the first couple of months, I cried at every service from beginning to end. It didn't matter what was happening, whether people were singing, preaching or praying . . . I was crying.

Then, during one service that spring, a song that I had heard before was sung by the choir, but this time, it hit differently. It was like I was hearing it for the first time; the lyrics from that song went from head knowledge and found its root in my heart. The song spoke about a King who loved me so much that He gave His life for me. It talked about how, in His love and in His death, I was forgiven and accepted after everything I had done and

> all the guilt and shame I was carrying. And I knew truly, for the first time in my life, that in this world, there will be no greater love that I will ever know than this love, the love of Jesus, the one who died to set me free of my guilt and shame.
>
> I decided THAT day to follow Him, give Him my life, and LET HIM write the story of my life because I was done writing my own story.
>
> Since that moment, I can tell you that this life I've been living is far more wonderful than anything I could have imagined. And this love I have, far greater than any other.

That is Exodus 20:2—understanding who God is and what He's done before you are given all the rules. In the book of Romans, we find what I believe is the New Testament equivalent of Exodus 20:2.

> For if while we were enemies we were reconciled to God through the death of His Son, much more, having been reconciled, we shall be saved by His life. (Romans 5:10 NASB)

Here is your 20-minute content: the death of Jesus Christ. When we say Christ died, that is a matter of history, but when we say Christ died for my sins, that is the gospel message. There is all the difference in the world between Jesus died and Jesus died for me. The former is an event; the latter is what interprets that event in my life. Let's see if it can become personal as we read a few verses prior.

> For while we were still helpless, at the right time Christ died for the ungodly. For one will hardly die for a righteous man; though perhaps for the good man someone would dare even to die. But God demonstrates His own love toward us, in that while we were yet sinners, Christ died

> for us. (Romans 5:6–8 NASB)

God "demonstrates" His love toward us. That word means He "proves it." He makes it conspicuous and plain, so clear that His love cannot be questioned. How does God prove His love toward us? Through Christ's death on the cross! He didn't save us by His teaching; He didn't save us by the Sermon on the Mount. Jesus had to die to save us. The cross is the supreme manifestation of His love. When you consider the cross, you see what price you are worth to God. Isn't it staggering to think you are worth the death of someone, and most staggering of all, that you are worth the death of God's Son?

Consider for a moment the kind of people Jesus died for. He didn't die for the wonderful; that would have been easy. Instead, notice the three terms Paul used: Jesus died for the helpless, the ungodly, and sinners. The helpless: totally unable in their own strength to please God. The ungodly: the people who are most unlike God. And sinners: those who cannot do anything to please God. And if that weren't enough, verse 10 adds one more name to the list:

> While we were enemies we were reconciled to God through the death of His Son. (Romans 5:10 NASB)

Enemies: man in his own nature is opposed to God because we love ourselves more than we love Him. God is the only God who loves His enemies. All other religions destroy their enemies; God loves them and died for them!

The word "reconciled" used here is profound. It means "a change in relationship between man and God." God's attitude toward us changed long before we changed our attitude about Him. He loves you just as you are, not as you should be. He didn't wait for you to change but chose to die for you when you were at your worst. He loves you in the condition that you are in, but He loves you so much that He won't let you remain in that condition.

So Jesus died for the helpless, ungodly, sinners, and enemies. That is why nobody can say they were born a Christian. That is impossible, for all have sinned. When Paul said in verse 7 that one "will hardly die for a righteous man, though perhaps for a good man, someone would even dare to die," he was asking: Would you die in the place of your children? Any parent would say, "Of course I would." I would always stand in my children's place to die for them. But then Paul amps it up to a whole other level. Would you die for someone who lied about you, posted something on social media about you, gossiped about you, stole from you? Paul essentially says, "This is what God has done."

I was on the subway recently and encountered a man going from car to car, begging for money. I gave him money. Some people are hesitant, asking all the questions: What will he spend it on? Cigarettes or drugs or alcohol? Is he scamming me? Personally, I consider what the Bible says: "He who gives to the poor lends to the Lord" (see Proverbs 19:17). I'm not here to be a detective. I'm here to love people, so I'm going to simply give. But let's change the story for a second. Let's say that my child was murdered a few weeks ago, and the man on the subway who is asking for money was the killer. Now what do I do? Let's say I don't even call the cops, but I show mercy and say, "I'm going to take you home and make you part of my family."

The thought of that seems outrageous! But that is exactly what God has done. We killed His Son. God found us as beggars and basically said, "You killed My Son, but instead of calling the cops or judging you, I'm going to give you what you never had before. I'm going to give you mercy and grace. I'm going to take you home and make you part of My family!" Mercy is God withholding the punishment we deserve for our sins, and grace is Him blessing us despite the fact that we don't deserve it. It's mindboggling to realize that when we get saved, we get all of Him. I have nothing to offer, but now that I'm in the family of God, He lives in me, and He makes me valuable. It is the deal of the century!

Let me explain it to you this way. I don't collect baseball cards anymore, but I have this one baseball card called Future Stars. Some say the card is worth $50, some even say it's worth $500. There are three players on this card. The first one is a guy named Jeff Schneider who played one year of professional baseball, pitched in 11 games and gave up 13 runs. Not impressive at all. The second player is named Bobby Bonner who played for four years, appeared in 61 games, had eight runs batted in and no home runs. And then there is a guy in the middle who played 21 years for the Orioles, appeared in 3,001 games—in fact played 2,632 consecutive games, beating Lou Gehrig's record—and came to bat 11,551 times. He got 3,184 hits, 431 homeruns and batted in 1,695 runs. His name is Cal Ripken, Jr. Now imagine you run into Bobby Bonner who boasts, “Hey, do you know that my card is worth $500?” Or Jeff Schneider proudly announcing, “I pitched 11 games, $500 for my card!”

You would laugh, knowing that the worth of the card has nothing to do with them. It’s the person they are connected to who gives value to their card. That's how it is when we come to Christ and point to our good works and our stats. “I'm a doctor. I'm a lawyer. I've made this much money. I've got a Tony Award, I've got this Oscar, I've got an MVP!” In reality, your card is probably worth about 30 cents. The real value comes from the one you are connected to—Jesus, who says, “I'm the one who died. I'm the one who set you free. I'm the one who did this for you!”

Now as Christians, we must not only consider what was accomplished through the death of Jesus but through the *life* of Jesus as well. Romans 5:10 goes on to say:

> For if while we were enemies we were reconciled to God through the death of His Son, *much more*, having been reconciled, we shall be saved by His life. (Romans 5:10 NASB, emphasis added)

What is that "much more" saying? If God reconciled us back to Himself through the death of Jesus when we were in that horrible state, how much *more* will He do for us now that we are His sons and daughters? In other words, if God gave His Son for us when we were public enemy number one, how much more will He do now that we are His own sons and daughters? He will do more, not less! What kind of father would help enemies and not help his own children?

So the next time someone asks you what God thinks about a controversial topic, you can say: "Before I can answer your question, I need to take 20 minutes to tell you who God is and what He has done for us." Read to them Romans 5:10, explaining how you were once helpless, ungodly, a sinner, and an enemy of God. "But God rescued me and changed me. If God did all this for me when I was in a horrible state, and He does much more now that I am His child, then my conclusion can only be: Whatever He asks or commands, there is no argument. I know He loves me, so I will obey!"

It reminds me of something I once read about Abraham Lincoln. Some years ago, I was fascinated with Lincoln and would read anything I could find that he had written. Lincoln ran for political office many times before becoming president. Throughout his life, he was outraged by the heinous crime of slavery that plagued America, and he was passionate to see it abolished.

It is said that when he was campaigning for one of his political positions, Lincoln heard about a slave auction happening nearby. Deeply indignant, he decided to go down to the slave block himself with one intention: to buy somebody and set them free. As the bidding went on for an 11-year-old girl, he also started bidding on her. As she looked at this tall white man bidding on her, she figured he was just like everybody else who wanted to buy and abuse her.

Lincoln would not be denied. He bid and won this young lady and then said, "Young lady, you are free."

"What does that mean?" she asked.

He looked at her and said, "It means you are free."

"Does that mean I can say whatever I want to say?" she asked.

He replied, "Yes, it does. You can say whatever you want to say."

"Does that mean that I can be whatever I want to be?" she continued.

Lincoln said, "You can be whatever you want to be."

"Does that mean I can go wherever I want to go?"

"Yes, you can go wherever you want to go," he answered.

With eyes streaming down her face, she said, "Then I shall go with you."[13]

She didn't ask what the rules were. She didn't ask what kind of house he lived in or what errands she would have to run. She simply said, "If you bought me, if you set me free, then I am yours today." This is the kind of response our hearts will have when we truly grasp what God has done for us. And instead of focusing on the rules, we need to point others to how God did the same for them—how He bought them, saved them, and set them free. And their glad response will be, "Then I shall go with You!"

STUCK UPSTAIRS WHEN I SHOULD BE DOWNSTAIRS

It is astonishing that many believers are unfamiliar with the Great Commission. Some have never heard of it at all. Yet the Bible clearly tells us that after His resurrection, Jesus gave us these specific instructions, defining our assignment here on earth:

Go therefore and make disciples of all the nations, baptizing them in the name of the Father and of the Son and of the Holy Spirit, teaching them to observe all things that I have commanded you; and lo, I am with you always, even to the end of the age. Amen. (Matthew 28:19-20 NKJV)

Hudson Taylor, the great Christian missionary who brought the gospel to China—a nation with close to 300 million believers now—said this: "The Great Commission is not an option to be considered; it is a command to be obeyed."[14] The Great Commission requires great faith and will challenge our comfort zones. Yet we must remember that evangelism is not a professional job reserved for a few trained men, rather it is the commission and responsibility of all those who call themselves the church. Leonard Ravenhill once made this thought-provoking statement: "Isn't it staggering when you think that one sermon on the day of Pentecost produced 3,000 people? And we have a city where 3,000 sermons are preached today and nobody was saved. And it doesn't even faze us."[15]

That's what happens when we are stuck upstairs when we should be downstairs.

What do I mean by that? As we take a brief look at the growth of Christianity from Acts 2 to Acts 4, it will begin to make sense. Acts 2 tells about the day of Pentecost when 120 people were praying in an upper room. Suddenly there was a magnificent visitation of the Holy Spirit, and they were all baptized, experiencing the power of the Holy Spirit. But the critical thing to note is that Acts 2 had to be followed by Acts 3. Acts 3 was the church leaving the upper room and leaving her comfort zone. That is when the work of God went downstairs and out onto the streets.

In other words, Acts 2 is the church service; Acts 3 is how billions come to Christ. After they came down the stairs from the upper room, Peter preached, and 3,000 came to Christ. Then in Acts 4, another 5,000 get saved. Eight thousand people came to Christ in a short period of time. Scholars have estimated that in the following years, Christianity began to grow at the rate of 40% each decade.[11] This Christian movement began to multiply all over the earth, bringing us to over 2 billion believers worldwide today. It excites my heart while at the same time presents a challenge, knowing that 5 billion people still don't know Christ.

I started reading an intriguing book titled *The Rise of Christianity: How the Obscure, Marginal Jesus Movement Became the Dominant Religious Force in the Western World in a Few Centuries*. The author, Rodney Stark, explains how the steady, rapid spread of Christianity was primarily due to the motivated efforts of the growing number of believers sharing the gospel with friends, relatives, and neighbors—not through a pulpit.[16] This is why I believe Acts chapters 2 and 3 are critical to understanding how we will win one billion souls. Our problem today is that we have people stuck upstairs when we should be downstairs. It's easy to lose sight of what our mission is. God put the Great Commission in the hands of each of us, not in pulpits around the world. I will be the first to admit that I am sometimes stuck upstairs when I should be downstairs. I get stuck in the church meeting and church building when I should be downstairs, where those 8,000 in the early church were.

I remember the first time when the consequences of being stuck upstairs hit me hard. It was years ago, when I was at Times Square Church as a guest speaker, and I was flying out of Newark Airport to return home. When I boarded the plane, they upgraded my seat to first class because of my frequent flyer status. I happily moved to seat 1A with nobody next to me. Thanking God for His favor, I got out my Bible, books, pen, paper, and even my music, ready to enjoy my quiet time with Jesus. Just as they were about to close the door, a guy wearing a hat and covered in tattoos very respectfully pointed to the seat beside me, saying, "Excuse me, that's my seat."

I was fuming. That was supposed to be Jesus's seat next to me on the flight! I had to pick up all my stuff, and I ended up sitting there listening to Christian music and reading the Bible with an attitude. Meanwhile, this guy just went to sleep for the entire flight. After we landed and taxied to the gate, everybody on the plane stood up, and suddenly I hear these ladies behind me say, "Hey, can we take a picture with you?"

"With me?" I asked.

"No, him!" they said, pointing to the guy who was sitting next to me. As they excitedly took pictures with him, I realized I had been sitting next to Kid Rock for two hours! But I was stuck upstairs when I should have been downstairs, missing a two-hour opportunity to share the gospel.

Thankfully the disciples went down the stairs. By the time we get to

Acts 3, a miracle takes place, leading to a message that sparked the multiplication of the church we are still experiencing today.

> Now Peter and John were going up to the temple at the ninth hour, the hour of prayer. And a certain man who had been lame from his mother's womb was being carried along, whom they used to set down every day at the gate of the temple which is called Beautiful, in order to beg alms of those who were entering the temple. And when he saw Peter and John about to go into the temple, he began asking to receive alms. And Peter, along with John, fixed his gaze upon him and said, "Look at us!" And he began to give them his attention, expecting to receive something from them. But Peter said, "I do not possess silver and gold, but what I do have I give to you: In the name of Jesus Christ the Nazarene—walk!" And seizing him by the right hand, he raised him up; and immediately his feet and his ankles were strengthened. And with a leap, he stood upright and began to walk; and he entered the temple with them, walking and leaping and praising God. And all the people saw him walking and praising God. (Acts 3:1-9 NASB)

Peter and John stepped out of their comfort zones and took a risk, praying for a lame man to be healed. That man's miraculous healing led to an additional 5,000 people getting saved!

> They were taking note of him as being the one who used to sit at the Beautiful Gate of the temple to beg alms, and they were filled with wonder and amazement at what had happened to him. While he was clinging to Peter and John, all the people ran together to them at the so-called portico of Solomon, full of amazement. (Acts 3:10-11 NASB)

The miracle of the lame man filled the people with wonder and amazement! It reminds me of a recent outreach that Pastor Carter Conlon and students from our Bible school did at Princeton University. During the time of worship that they held on the college campus, a guy suddenly started running around, crying out, "I'm healed! I'm healed! I'm healed!" There were many bystanders, a number of them Muslims. They watched the worship, the prayer meeting, the preaching, and saw all the people rejoicing. One of them commented, "All of you seem warm and glowy. We don't know what this is!" As they reached the end of their meeting at Princeton, many students were getting saved right there on campus. A foreign exchange student came over and saw all these people jumping and worshipping God and asked, "Why is everybody dancing and so happy?"

When people find Jesus, they find joy, and an outbreak of joy attracts the bystanders. As the people ran with excitement to Solomon's colonnade, Peter saw his opportunity and began to address the crowd (see Acts 3:12). Picture the scene: here is Peter preaching to thousands of people with a man hanging onto him. One man preached, the other was the object lesson—and it was enough to bring 5,000 to Christ. What we don't need today are preachers bringing up all the props in the book. Just bring up people who have been saved! Bring up miraculous testimonies, and watch what begins to happen in church.

Many don't realize this, but my seminary—all my homiletics and hermeneutics courses, all my training to preach—came at 19 years old when I was placed in a prostitution hotel every Thursday night. Every Thursday night for five years, I preached to pimps and prostitutes. During the first Bible study we ever had, two people got saved: Travis the pimp and Radio the hitman. Travis was the pimp in the hotel. Radio was the "hitman" not because he was killing people but because if you gave him $25, he would get you a bag of heroin and knew where to stick the needle to get you high. Those were the first two miracles, and they sat in the front row of this prostitution hotel for five years as proof that Jesus can change lives. Those guys were my lame men.

Peter's sermon was very simple. Without going into details, his four-part sermon was essentially him telling the people: You denied Jesus and desired other people (see Acts 3:14). If you put your faith in His name, you can have a miracle (verse 16). Repent and be converted so that your sins may be forgiven (verse 19). To reject this is to perish into eternity (verse 23). It was that simple, and at the conclusion of it, 5,000 people believed and got saved (see Acts 4:4).

Imagine what would have happened if the disciples stayed in the upper room and never came downstairs. You would have 120 people singing the same songs and telling the same stories over and over again. When you stay upstairs, you are forced to start coming up with weird stuff to try to keep things exciting. Yet the most exciting thing that can happen in a meeting is getting a lame man walking, and people coming from darkness into light. That's what God wants to do!

We recently took a team down to Grenada and ministered in the prisons, to pastors, and to the people. What God did was absolutely amazing. We were told that the building we met in had never been full for a church service, yet we had about a thousand people show up for the night of worship! At four o'clock, we worshipped with and ministered to over a hundred leaders, with standing room only. It was amazing to speak to these pastors and leaders in Grenada, but the thing that ignited my soul happened earlier at eleven o'clock when we went into the prison.

There were 400 inmates in the only prison in Grenada, ranging from those who had stolen to those who had committed murder.

We walked through all the security and several gates before entering what felt like walking into old Jerusalem—with three-story buildings, stairs coming down, bars on windows. We met the warden of the prison, and I was surprised when he said to me, "Good to see you! I listen to TSC every morning and night on the radio. I drive in listening to TSC, I drive home listening to TSC!" This man who oversees 400 inmates loves Jesus. I asked what we could do for him, and he wanted 400 copies of one of my books to give to all the inmates in the prison!

We set up a tent outside, and I watched an anointing fall on our worship leaders, Willie and Ricardo. They played and sang like never before, and my heart leapt within me. It felt like I was returning to my roots, remembering how I spent my first seven years preaching on the streets. Inmates sat on stairs in front of us, peering out from behind the bars, and more listened from beyond another gate. They were captivated by the worship. I began to preach the gospel, telling them about God's willingness to rewrite their story and offer them a second chance. The prisoners locked in at that moment, and I knew it was nothing but the Holy Ghost. It was exciting to hear the prisoners cry out to God for a miracle and then watch them become born again. Preaching to pastors and Christians can easily turn into upper room ministry, but preaching in prisons or to people that everyone wants to bypass—that's going to the ground level.

So what does a ground-floor Christian look like? It is someone who is willing to leave his comfort zone and come downstairs, someone who is not satisfied merely sitting in church on Sundays. Here are three things to keep in mind regarding ground-floor Christians:

1. GOD USES 3 P.M. CHRISTIANS.

Look once again at verse 1 of Acts 3:

> Now Peter and John were going up to the temple at the ninth hour, the hour of prayer. (Acts 3:1 NASB)

In the Jewish religious system, the ninth hour refers to 3 P.M. The ninth hour was when they would normally go to prayer. In other words, God was putting them back on schedule. He never intended for the disciples to remain in the upper room. Instead, they became what I call "3 P.M. Christians." 3 P.M. Christians are people who were touched by the Holy Spirit in a special setting but now take that new touch and bring it to their everyday environments. The disciples started attending the normal prayer meeting instead of the upper room prayer meeting. Just as Acts 3 determined if Acts 2 was real, real life will determine whether or not what we have received is real.

Today it would be God touching you on a Sunday at church, and then you being used on Monday through Saturday. A 3 P.M. Christian comes to the same everyday setting but with a different heart and a different perspective. God doesn't change our places. He changes the person and then sends them back to the same place to get back on their daily schedule.

That is what happened after we held those three services in Grenada. As powerful as our time in Grenada was, what was interesting to me was flying back to New York the next day after everything was over. Sitting in an exit row was Cindy, Ricardo, and myself, and every time the flight attendant would come near us, we would talk to her. We would begin to make conversation, laugh together, and at one point we asked, "Do you go to church?"

Her answer surprised us. "I looked up your names in the back there, and while I looked up your names, I ordered your book! And then I realize that you guys are online. I've been going to church only because my little daughter keeps bringing me."

Suddenly she brought over another flight attendant who said, "I used to live in New York and I used to go to Times Square Church!"

And right there at 30,000 feet in the air, Cindy, Ricardo, and I took their hands and prayed for them.

Why did we have to do it there? We prayed for them before we landed because those flight attendants could not come to church—the church needed to come to them. The church needed to be on JetBlue flight 350. Consider how in Acts 3, the man who gets healed and saved was a lame man. Remember, this miracle takes place on the ground. In Acts 2, the church was in the upper room, but that lame man could not walk up those stairs. The only way a miracle happens is if the church comes down the stairs with their good legs instead of saying, "We'll sit in our church and wait for you to come and see us." No! God has people who need to be saved on JetBlue and on the streets of your city. We must realize that the church cannot stand still.

If the disciples don't go into Jerusalem, then Pentecost becomes meaningless. If you don't bring the church into your community, then your services are for naught. Pentecost was not meant to create more Pentecost, but just the occasional Pentecost—like in Acts 4:4 when the believers met for a prayer meeting on account of persecution. The place where they had gathered was shaken, and they were all filled with the Holy Spirit, just like in Acts 2. In other words, the upper room is a filling station, not a residence hall. Sometimes we need to go and get filled with the Holy Spirit, but we don't live there because there are JetBlue flight attendants and beggars who need to be healed and set free.

I love that God never memorialized the upper room. Did you notice that after Acts 2, no one ever returned to the upper room? They didn't set up a souvenir shop or make it a tourist attraction where they proudly pointed out the burn marks on the floor. They didn't sell admission tickets to the upper room because that was not where the power was. The power came on the ground with the laymen.

Some people assume that if you stop the upper room, you stop the whole move of God. But when they came down those stairs, the church wasn't canceled. The church simply moved because the church is living, and living things move.

2. GOD WILL GIVE YOU NEW EYES WHEN YOU COME DOWNSTAIRS.

When you come downstairs, the ordinary suddenly starts to look like candidates for the extraordinary. That lame man wasn't new. In Acts 3, it says he had been put there every day since he was a child, which means Peter and John passed that man probably dozens, maybe a hundred times before.

When he saw Peter and John about to go into the temple, he asked them for alms as usual. I wonder how many times they ignored him in the past because they had heard the same cry over and over. But all of a sudden when God touches you, you will not only love God more, you will love people more as well.

It's not a true work of God if you don't treat people better after receiving a touch of God. After passing by this lame man every day, Peter and John were finally truly seeing him. The ordinary and the common started to look different. That is what should happen after you leave church on Sunday. You should begin to see through Jesus's eyes—from people on the streets to your spouse, your kids, your coworkers.

What do we do with our new eyes? Pray with people as much as possible! I challenge you to begin noticing the people around you, and then ask this question whenever you can: “Can I pray with you?” In my 42 years of ministry and asking that question, only three people at the most declined the offer.

Great revivals send missionaries. Great revivals become evangelistic because suddenly God’s people are seeing with new eyes. When they keep boasting about how many days they've had a revival, it's a sure sign that it is about to die. I was reading about the Azusa Street Revival, which was an upper room experience that hit our country in 1906 on Azusa Street in Los Angeles. God used a one-eyed preacher named William Seymour. Within five months of this outpouring of the Holy Spirit, 38 missionaries left Azusa Street with new eyes. In two years, they were in 50 nations worldwide. By 1910 when everything was done, Azusa had 200 Pentecostal missionaries who went abroad![17]

God uses 3 P.M. Christians who come downstairs and begin seeing with new eyes. Finally, we must remember that . . .

3. THE BAPTISM OF THE HOLY SPIRIT CHANGES EVERYTHING.

D. L. Moody, the great American evangelist, is thought to have personally led one million people to Jesus. He made a covenant with God that he would lead at least one person a day to Jesus. There were nights when he would go to bed and realize he hadn't spoken to anybody that day. He would then get out of bed, get dressed, and go find some unsuspecting soul on the street with whom to start sharing the gospel.

How did D. L. Moody personally lead a million people to Christ? It is said that by age 62, he preached face-to-face to a hundred million people. He acknowledged when it all changed:

> I remember two holy women who used to come to my meetings. When I began to preach, I could tell by the expression on their faces that they were praying for me. At the close of the Sunday evening service they would say to me, "We have been praying for you."
>
> I said, "Why don't you pray for the people?"
>
> They answered, "You need power."

> "I need power?" I said to myself. "Why, I thought I had power."
>
> I had a large Sunday school and the largest congregation in Chicago. But right along, these two godly women kept praying for me. I asked them to come and talk with me, and we got down on our knees. They poured out their hearts that I might receive the anointing from the Holy Spirit, and there came a great hunger into my soul. I did not know what it was. I began to pray as I never did before. I really felt that I did not want to live if I could not have this power for service. The hunger increased. I was praying all the time that God would fill me with His Holy Spirit.
>
> Well, one day in the city of New York–oh, what a day! I cannot describe it. I seldom refer to it; it is almost too sacred an experience to name. I can only say that God revealed Himself to me, and I had such an experience of His love that I asked Him to stay His hand.
>
> I went to preaching again. The sermons were not different, I did not present any new truths; and yet hundreds were converted.[18]

Don't miss the power of the Holy Spirit! The Holy Spirit was not given to you so you could stay in the upper room for revival services. The Holy Spirit was given to you to walk down the stairs.

Recently we had Nicky Cruz—the gang member who was radically saved and whose story is told in *The Cross and the Switchblade*—preach at our church. Even at 86 years old, he speaks with as much passion as if he just got saved last week! Together, he and I attended the funeral of Sonny Arguinzoni, the first drug addict delivered and saved in the Teen Challenge program in Brooklyn. As a result of Sonny Arguinzoni's salvation and graduation from

Teen Challenge, 700 Victory Outreach centers in 35 states and 400 churches were started.[19]

It is incredible to think that Nicky Cruz, Sonny Arguinzoni, Teen Challenge, *The Cross and the Switchblade*, Victory Outreach, World Challenge, and Times Square Church were all birthed from the heart and the burden of David Wilkerson. None of this started because David Wilkerson had a vision of Teen Challenge or thought, “I’m going to write a bestseller.” It all started with the idea of turning off his TV at night and spending that time in prayer. As a result, he was led to New York City to reach the hearts of the toughest gangsters on the streets—not with his own expertise or charisma, but simply through the power of the Holy Spirit. Some people are waiting for an earth-shattering vision when what we need to do is listen to the whisper of the Holy Spirit for the simplest thing. *Turn this off. Don't do that. Use this time to pray.* Don't think gigantic. Just ask, “Holy Spirit, what are You saying to me right now?”

Don’t get stuck upstairs. Come downstairs and be a 3 P.M. Christian, allowing God to use you where He placed you. Instead of complaining about where you are, ask God to help you see people with new eyes. And finally, ask God to fill you with the Holy Spirit every morning, knowing that the Holy Spirit changes everything!

05

THE FISH ARE FOUND IN THE DEEP

Everyone loves a good story, but the best ones rarely come easily. By the end of this chapter, my hope is that you will find yourself yearning for your own "fish story." Of course, if you want a fish story, it's important to remember that fish are always found in the deep.

Now I'm not referring to literal fish stories about how the big one got away. The best way to explain what I mean by a "deep sea fishing" story is to give you an example. Recently, Cindy and I joined Nicky and Gloria Cruz in attending the funeral of Sonny Arguinzoni. Sonny was the first drug addict saved and delivered at Teen Challenge. When we walked into the Peacock Theater in Los Angeles, the same venue that hosts the Grammys, we found 7,000 people gathered to honor this man of God.

The curtain opened, and a 300-voice choir composed of people who have been set free by the power of Christ began to sing the praises of God. I imagine that the Peacock Theater never heard singing and music like that before. It was the joyful celebration of how God used Sonny to plant 700 Victory Outreach centers and 400 churches in 35 countries. We saw video clips of the impact of these ministries, and it was overwhelming to see what God is doing from Mexico City to Amsterdam to South Africa as well as right here in the United States.

Sonny's salvation story is an extraordinary one—a deep sea fishing story—recounted by David Wilkerson in his book *Beyond the Cross and the Switchblade*:

> I met Sonny not long after I found Shorty and his friends on the rooftop of my Second Avenue Trysting Place, swishing hypodermic needles in a Coca-Cola bottle full of dirty water, and determined that I would not preach again until I was certain I had something to say. I found young Sonny leaning against a lamppost beneath an elevated train in the Bedford-Stuyvesant district of Brooklyn. I remember that there was a pizza store nearby.
>
> The poor kid—he must have weighed every bit of 120 pounds. His eyes were sunken, dark, as if someone had hit him. He stood lolling up against the post, so drowsy that he seemed to be dropping to sleep as I tried to talk to him. At first Sonny would have nothing to do with me. He thought I was a narcotics agent. When I suggested a pizza however—I remember I said I'd buy him a pepperoni—he brightened just a little. We ate with me doing a monologue and with Sonny dozing. I said I'd come back another day, and if I found him around, I'd try anchovies with him next.
>
> Well, over pizzas, Sonny and I gradually came to know each other, though it was clear Sonny still wondered what I was up to. Then one day I let it out that I was going to be holding a service in a small Puerto Rican church in the neighborhood. None of Sonny's junkie friends wanted to miss that—a narco trying to pull off a sermon. There were two things wrong with that: I wasn't a narcotics agent, and I wasn't going to preach, I was going to put myself out on a limb with a promise. Come to Jesus and His Spirit will free you of your addiction.

The day for the service came. Gang members sporting incongruous Alpine hats and carrying canes, junkies strung out on heroin, their girls, all sorts and conditions of kids flocked into the little church that night to see the show. At the end of the praise service I gave an altar call. A small group of junkies came forward, including Sonny. I told him that I felt God had His hand on him and I asked him if he would come stay with Gwen and me until God had done His work. Sonny came along in a half stupor. I'll never forget my introduction to "cold turkey" withdrawal. That night I watched as Sonny's legs jerked violently and perspiration soaked his pajamas. One moment he shivered from cold, and the next he threw back his covers trying to shake off hot flashes. Goose bumps which made him look like a dressed fowl were visible all over his arms and neck.

I needed to go to Brooklyn on one of the following days, and I didn't want to leave Sonny alone, so I asked him if he'd come along. As soon as we crossed the bridge, I noticed the boy's restlessness return. Suddenly he was crying, "Let me out! It's no use. I've got to have a fix." I tried to argue with him, but he opened the car door when I came to a light and leaped from the car.

So Sonny went back on drugs!

I remember talking to Gwen about whether I should quit and go back to Phillipsburg. "I don't see what I can do here," I said. "I failed with Sonny."

"Now Dave," said Gwen, "in the first place, I'm sure you're never going to have 100 percent success: you've got to work with more boys before you can make a decision. And beyond that," she smiled, "how do you know what Christ may have in mind for Sonny?"

Gwen was right. The Lord did have something special in mind for Sonny, but He had to wait for the boy to get desperate first. That took several months. But then Sonny got himself into trouble. He was getting further addicted. He ran out of money, started to steal, and once was shot in the leg. More months passed during which I lost track of the boy while he was sinking further into his private hell.

In the meanwhile, we had launched our work at Teen Challenge and had a few successes. Among them was a fan boy named Chino who had once been a friend of Sonny Arguinzoni. Later we learned about the day Chino ran into Sonny, lolling as usual around a street corner. "Hey, man," said Sonny, "good to see you out."

Sonny assumed that Chino had been in prison because he no longer had the tight look of a man strung out on heroin. But Chino had another story. He told Sonny how Christ had pulled him out of the pit and saved him. Of course, Sonny didn't believe him. Chino invited Sonny to go with him to the Teen Challenge Center in Brooklyn. Sonny accepted with the thought that the center must be some sort of dance club.

Sonny ended up fully committing his life to Christ, and the next day he realized that this center had been founded by the same "skinny country preacher" who once had taken him into his home. In Sonny's case the Holy Spirit waited for that moment of desperation, before He reached inside the boy's soul and transformed it.

But transform it He did.[20]

Because of Sonny's transformed life, tens of thousands of young men and women have been saved and delivered all over the world. That's not just a story, it's a fish story. It's a big fish story, and these kinds are only found in deep waters. We as the church must remember that we exist primarily for those who do not know Jesus yet. When the church becomes self-consuming, thinking that it's all about us, we have missed our reason for existence. Those who are not saved yet is why the words "soul-winning evangelism" and "deep sea fishing" are so important. The statistic that I read recently said that every six times the gospel is shared, one person will receive Christ. The challenge is for us to truly grasp how important this is.

Reflecting on Sonny's life and stories, attending the funeral with Nicky Cruz who is 86, remembering David Wilkerson, and even considering Billy Graham's daughter, Anne Graham Lotz, who recently spoke at our church—I can't help but feel an acute awareness that these men and women, who have sacrificed so much and left an incredible legacy, are all growing older and will soon be with the Lord. I believe the question we ought to consider is not merely "What's next for the church?" but "Who is next?" Who will God use? Who will say, "Here am I, send me"? God is writing a new story for His people and His church. I grew up hearing all the old stories, but heaven is waiting to write new ones. Yet many times the delay is caused by those who hesitate to say yes to God.

For a thousand years, the children of Israel had been telling the same story about God delivering them from Egypt. They would say, "Have you heard about Moses and Joshua, the parting of the Red Sea, the falling of the walls of Jericho?" But after a thousand years, they suddenly hear the prophet Jeremiah say, "Those stories have an expiration date. There is a new story God wants you to tell." This is what he prophesied:

> "Therefore behold, days are coming," declares the Lord,

> "when it will no longer be said, 'As the Lord lives, who brought up the sons of Israel out of the land of Egypt,' but, 'As the Lord lives, who brought up the sons of Israel from the land of the north and from all the countries where He had banished them.'" (Jeremiah 16:14–15 NASB)

What was this new story of the north that they would be telling? Jeremiah was saying, "God rescued you from Egypt. That was the old story. But there is a new story coming, and you will tell of how God set you free from Babylon to rebuild the temple and the wall." Babylon and Persia were the lands of the north, the new stories that were about to unfold.

God was saying, "You will tell your children new stories about what I am doing. There will be new scenarios, new characters, new miracles. You will talk about three teenage boys named Shadrach, Meshach and Abednego in the north who refused to bow to a 90-foot idol, even though they were threatened with a fiery furnace. And when they were thrown into that fiery furnace, there was a fourth man in the fire with them!

"You will tell the story of a bartender in Persia named Nehemiah who started to cry before a king when he heard about the state of his nation, Israel. The heathen king ends up sending Nehemiah back home to rebuild a wall and eventually become the governor of Jerusalem.

"You will hear about a young man named Daniel who, though the government set up laws forbidding prayer to anyone but the king, would open up his window and continue to pray to God. As punishment, he was thrown into a lion's den, but those lions' mouths were shut tight; they wouldn't even touch Daniel. Instead, those who conspired against him were thrown in, and that's when God opened the mouths of the lions.

"You will tell about a priest named Ezra who was in captivity yet returned to Jerusalem to rebuild the temple. You will hear about a woman in government against all odds—a Jewish woman named Esther who became queen and put her life on the line to stop a genocide. You are going to tell so many new stories because I'm not a God who is stuck in the past. I just need people to say yes!"

By the time we get to the New Testament, we see the potential for even more new stories with the unlikeliest of people—fishermen who are challenged to fish in a different way:

> Now it happened that while the crowd was pressing around [Jesus] and listening to the word of God, He was standing by the lake of Gennesaret; and He saw two boats lying at the edge of the lake; but the fishermen had gotten out of them and were washing their nets. And He got into one of the boats, which was Simon's, and asked him to put out a little way from the land. And He sat down and began teaching the people from the boat. When He had finished speaking, He said to Simon, "Put out into the deep water and let down your nets for a catch." Simon answered and said, "Master, we worked hard all night and caught nothing, but I will do as You say and let down the nets." When they had done this, they enclosed a great quantity of fish, and their nets began to break; so they signaled to their partners in the other boat for them to come and help them. And they came and filled both of the boats, so that they began to sink. But when Simon Peter saw that, he fell down at Jesus' feet, saying, "Go away from me Lord, for I am a sinful man!" For amazement had seized him and all his companions because of the catch of fish which they had taken; and so also were James and John, sons of Zebedee, who were partners with Simon. And Jesus said to Simon, "Do not fear, from now on you will be catching

> men." When they had brought their boats to land, they left everything and followed Him. (Luke 5:1–11 NASB)

The purpose of the 12 disciples was not to go fishing for fish but to fish for men. Jesus was beginning to course correct what their purpose was. Fishing for men is evangelism and soul-winning, and the assignment hasn't changed for us as His followers today. That's why no matter what God has gifted you to do and no matter where He has placed you—in sports, politics, finance, education, medicine, or whatever it may be—there is a much bigger purpose for you than a paycheck, career, or retirement plan. God has strategically placed you in a fishing hole. I believe you are there for at least one person who is headed to hell but now can have the opportunity to go to heaven. Wherever a Christian is placed, it's because someone there needs to be saved; they need you! You are there to go fishing and to see people come to Christ. Don't forget your true purpose.

I was reading a fascinating story about the largest tomb in the world: the Taj Mahal. It was one of the most beautiful and costly tombs ever built. When the favorite wife of the Indian ruler died in 1631, he ordered that a magnificent tomb be built as a memorial for her. The Shah placed his wife's casket in the middle of the property of land, and construction of the tomb was to begin all around it. The construction of the main building, the Taj Mahal and Agra, lasted more than 20 years. They did not finish it until 1653. Several years into the venture, the Shah's grief over his late wife started to give way to passion for the building of this glorious structure. It is said that while he was coming on the site, he looked at the middle and saw the wooden box and asked, "What is that? Throw that out!"[21]

It was the casket! He got so blown away with how beautiful the building was that he forgot why he was doing it in the first place. We as the church exist so people can get saved, not so we can get followers and become famous. We are here so we can populate heaven by the gospel of Jesus Christ. But in many ways, we've thrown out the casket. We've thrown out what matters—the gospel and souls being saved. We must not lose our original purpose as the church.

The passage we looked at in Luke 5 reminds us of our purpose by showing us three possible places we can find ourselves in the story: on land with the listeners, in the shallows, or in the deep. What do each of these places represent?

The people on land are listening to Jesus. I believe we all need to be on land to hear the Word of God.

The people in the shallows are helping the multitude hear Jesus. Notice that Peter used his boat, pushed out just a little bit, and in doing so, enabled the multitude to hear Jesus more easily. Most of us want to serve in the church to make it easier for people to listen in the shallows. Ushers, the worship team, children's workers, hospitality—everyone plays a vital role. But at some point, the Lord will challenge you to push away from the shore to fish for people who have never heard Him before.

That brings us to the people in the deep—those who are co-laboring with Jesus. They believe there are others who should be on land listening to the Lord but have yet to be brought in. Finding those fish is the primary reason for their existence, and that is why they are willing to launch out into the deep.

Looking again at the passage in Luke 5, I want to highlight some words in verses 2 and 3.

> He saw two boats. (verse 2)
>
> He got into one of the boats. (verse 3)

I cannot help but wonder: Would Jesus have picked my boat?

Would He have chosen me to be used by God?

There are always two boats ready, but if you want to be chosen, it starts with the cry, "Pick my boat. Use me! Do something through me!" It is being convinced that you don't want to go to heaven alone and choosing to put out into the deep. If that is you—you are eager for your own fish story—then here are a few things to keep in mind that will help you be prepared for deep sea fishing.

1. YOU NEED OBEDIENCE.

Deep sea fishing requires obedience, and the challenge is to remain obedient even when you don't understand. You can expect to be asked to move out of your comfort zone, just like Peter had to. Peter tried to explain to Jesus that they had been fishing all night to no avail. I can imagine what must have been going through his mind. "A carpenter is telling me, the fisherman, the best place and time to fish? He deals with wood; I'm the one who deals with fish." Just like Peter, we tend to rely on our experience instead of His omniscience.

Our experience might tell us to keep quiet so we don't get into trouble at work, or not to mention the gospel because this person is not ready to hear it just yet. Instead, we must learn to rely on Him! After all, can the catcher, a fish himself, really be smarter than the creator of the fish? Jesus can easily stand in the boat and command, "Fish, come right over here." He can do whatever He wants!

Peter ended up making the right choice even though it made no logical sense to him. He said to Jesus, "I will do as You say." God will often ask you to do things that don't make sense, but He is God, and you are not. Rely on omniscience, not experience. Rely on the mind of God, not your logical conclusions.

Many years ago, I saw a movie called *We Bought a Zoo*, based on the true story of a British writer named Benjamin Mee who rescued a failing zoo while coming to terms with the fact that he was a widower. There is this one line from the movie that always gets me. When they asked him why he was saving the zoo, he said, "Sometimes all you need is 20 seconds of insane courage."[22] There will be times when we just need to say, "I don't know what I'm doing, but You are God, and I'm not. I'm just going to do what You've asked me to do." That's what gets you into the deep waters. That's what got David Wilkerson speaking to Nicky Cruz and Sonny Arguinzoni. Fish stories are in the deep, but we don't go there naturally. It is obedience that gets us there.

For many years, the actual fishing industry has ranked in the top two of the most dangerous industries to work in, alternating spots with logging. Spiritually speaking, I believe it is still the most dangerous thing to be a part of. After all, the one in six who gets saved each have the potential of bringing many people to Christ. Satan will oppose every effort that he can. David Wilkerson almost lost his life while deep sea fishing in the gangs of New York. He was slapped and threatened to be killed. Satan fought hard against Nicky getting saved so he wouldn't speak to 50 million people. He got Sonny to jump out of a car on the Brooklyn Bridge so 700 centers would not exist to set young people free from drugs and alcohol. Nevertheless, God is relentless to bring these people to Himself. All He needs is obedient men and women.

I was reading the story of Steve Jobs when he started Apple. In 1982, Jobs invited John Sculley, the president of PepsiCo at that time, to be the chief financial officer. Apple wasn't well known yet, leaving Sculley hesitant. He had a sweet deal in Atlanta with Pepsi and didn't need to make a move. But Jobs looked at him and asked, "Do you want to sell sugar water the rest of your life, or do you want to come with me and change the world?"

Sculley said that moment felt as if someone delivered a blow to his stomach. "The question was a monstrous one, for which I had no answer. It knocked the wind out of me." After Jobs posed that question, Sculley packed his bags and moved west, and the rest is history.[23]

We are not called to bring sugar water Christianity; we are called to change the world. But in order to allow God to do something amazing through us, we must venture into the deep—where it's dangerous, but where the fish are.

2. YOU NEED NETS.

Not only is obedience required, you will also need nets. Catching fish in a lake requires nets, but to fish in your community, on your job, in your country, you will need a different kind of net. The fish in the world need us to open up our mouth. These are our nets today:

> How then shall they call upon Him in whom they have not believed? And how shall they believe in Him whom they have not heard? And how shall they hear without a preacher? (Romans 10:14 NASB)

They need to hear your voice speaking truth. Paul goes on to say:

> So faith comes from hearing, and hearing by the word of Christ. But I say, surely they have never heard, have they? (Romans 10:17–18 NASB)

When it comes to witnessing, the gospel is spoken, and the gospel is heard. That is the net. We use our nets when we open our mouths and speak God's truth. For years we have missed it, assuming that if we got lights and smoke and gave people coffee in our churches, we would catch fish, when in reality, it is the gospel spoken that catches fish.

It is concerning that according to recent statistics, 95% of all Christians have never won a soul to Christ. Eighty percent of all Christians do not consistently witness for Christ. Less than 2% are involved in the ministry of evangelism, and 71% percent do not give toward the financing of the Great Commission.[24] We must understand that to be silent or scared as the church is not an option. The world needs a serious and sold-out church today who is not afraid to speak, regardless of what consequences may be.

I have noticed over the years that the church has lost her voice even in the sanctuary. Clapping has replaced us opening up our mouths. No one says "amen" anymore but instead we have learned to merely clap in agreement. Ezra was part of those new stories of the north, and notice what the people in his day did:

> And Ezra opened the book in the sight of all the people for he was standing above all the people; and when he opened it, all the people stood up. Then Ezra blessed the Lord the great God. And all the people answered, "Amen, Amen!" while lifting up their hands; then they bowed low and worshiped the Lord with their faces to the ground. (Nehemiah 8:5–6 NASB)

When Ezra blessed the Lord, did the people respond by clapping? No, they said, "Amen!" I challenge you in your church services, whether during worship or the preaching, to say, "Amen! Hallelujah!" If you don't sing or speak in church, it is likely that you are not witnessing either because your mouth is being trained to remain shut. Notice this command in the Bible:

> Let the redeemed of the Lord say so, whom He has redeemed from the hand of the adversary. (Psalm 107:2 NASB)

If God set you free from the enemy, the Bible doesn't tell you to clap but to say so! The NLT says it this way: "Has the Lord redeemed you? Then speak out! Tell others he has redeemed you from your enemies" (Psalm 107:2).

The power is in our voice. It is part of preaching, evangelism, testimony, singing, agreement, and praying. None of those things can be done by clapping. We must open up our mouths. I encourage you to train yourself to fight this battle of opening up your mouth by praising Him. Bring your "amen" and "hallelujah" and "Jesus is Lord" in church, and it will help you to open your mouth outside as well. Fish don't get caught unless they receive truth, and they don't receive truth unless you speak.

To go deep sea fishing, you need obedience, you need nets, and finally . . .

3. YOU NEED HELP.

Winning souls requires many of the same skills as being a fisherman. You won't catch fish unless you go where the fish are. You can stay close to the shore, or you can put out into the deep. One gets sermons, the other gets fish. The deep is where the fish are, and being out there requires patience, just like in real fishing. Out in the deep is where the catches can be so great that they cause the nets to break, which means that you will need help. The disciples' fishing expedition resulted in so many fish that their nets began to break, and they needed another boat to come help.

A well-known evangelist once said, "It takes about ten people to lead someone to Christ. Someone praying, someone witnessing, someone being an example."[25] Peter got the miracle, and the other boat got the overflow. Here is the Apostle Paul's take on the Billy Graham "ten":

> What then is Apollos? And what is Paul? Servants through whom you believed, even as the Lord gave opportunity to each one. I planted, Apollos watered, but God was causing the growth. So then neither the one who plants nor the one who waters is anything, but God who causes the growth. Now he who plants and he who waters are one; but each

> will receive his own reward according to his own labor. For we are God's fellow workers. (1 Corinthians 3:5–9 NASB)

An unnamed woman went deep sea fishing among the homeless in Manhattan, and the result was the emergence of a powerful prayer warrior named Maria. And just as Paul said, we also see a number of other people involved in bringing Maria to Jesus. Here is her story:

> My sixth birthday was supposed to be the happiest day of my life. I remember my mother, who had gotten beautiful fabric from the United States, made me a special dress. But that day marked the beginning of a profound change.
>
> I was molested by a family friend. I was in shock. When my mother found me in the bathroom, instead of asking what was wrong, she assumed I'd been trying to ride the broken bicycle in front of our building. It was a rusted frame with no tires, the one she'd always warned me to stay away from. "Didn't I tell you not to get on that bike? You're going to get cut!" she scolded, and spanked me so hard my body shook. I was too terrified to speak. I carried that secret for years, a secret that filled me with shame. I'd overhear the old ladies talking about how only virgins wore white dresses at their weddings, and I knew that wouldn't be me.
>
> I lost my way during my teenage years. I dropped out of school and had three children before I turned twenty: two boys, whom my mother raised, and a beautiful girl whom I gave up for adoption. I lived on the streets, eventually becoming homeless and sleeping in a cardboard box.
>
> Then a woman of God from TSC, sent on a divine mission, would visit the homeless people. Sometimes, I think she was an angel. She'd bring a bottle of rubbing alcohol, a pair

of socks, a peanut butter sandwich, and a message: "God doesn't want you to die." But I did. So she said, "Then we must prepare you for death. You can't go to heaven like this." Little did I know she was preparing me to live, and for my old self to die.

I remember the first time I fell asleep on the sidewalk without my shoes and woke up to find them gone. After that, I slept with my shoes on, but they caused red sores and blisters. My socks would stick to the bleeding wounds on the bottom of my feet. With immense love, she would wash my feet. That became one of the biggest testimonies of my life. Things began to change. When I had money, the drug spots would be closed.

I decided to go to church, but as I approached the building, I saw police officers and panicked. I knew they probably recognized me; sleeping on the streets was illegal. I was overcome with shame. I wanted a new life, a place where no one knew my past, but I didn't know how to achieve it. I wanted my pain, my sin, washed away. I wanted to be born again, but I still had the same question: how could a grown person be born again?

Instead of going into TSC, I walked toward Broadway. People were running, so I ran, and I was arrested. When I asked the officer why, he said, "Why were you running?" The next day in court, the judge offered me an opportunity. "Is that your family?" she asked, pointing to a woman behind me. I turned and saw a lady who said, "I'm praying for you." In my next court appearance, I was mandated to a program. I graduated, got a city job, and moved to the Bronx. I didn't want to return to Manhattan. I felt God had taken me from that area, but I lacked faith. I didn't understand God's power, but I wanted to serve Him. I joined a small Pentecostal church.

About six months later, during a foot-washing ceremony, I thought, "Oh my God, I have to get my feet done; they have to look good." When I was called to the altar, the elder took my feet and began speaking in tongues. I understood what she was saying: "God has been washing your feet all along." We both felt the presence of the Holy Spirit. God revealed that He was the one washing my feet with alcohol, feeding me peanut butter sandwiches, and restoring my life. I hadn't even realized it, just like the disciples who walked with Jesus without fully understanding.

Fast forward, I retired after 28 years with the city. God restored my family. We had a reunion. I met my daughter at the age of 23. I have nine grandchildren. My youngest son, has a special gift, teaching me unconditional love and trust in God. When he was about to join the adult service at our Spanish-speaking church, I realized he wouldn't understand the sermons. I spoke to the pastor, but he told me to find another church. So, I returned to TSC, the place I thought I couldn't serve God because of the environment. But God changed everything. He changed me.

One Tuesday, Pastor Carter preached about God's new name, and I heard "Martha." I cried, remembering Martha's busyness and lack of time for Jesus. The next day, in my prayer closet, I heard God say, "My servant." I remembered a time I'd translated at Woodycrest nursing home, which serves residents with AIDS, HIV, and addictions. I contacted them, and despite the initial contact being unavailable, I called the nursing home. I asked to come in and teach a Bible class once a week, and

> the director agreed. Walking in, I felt God's presence. I remembered the woman from TSC's words: "God will restore." I wanted to cry, but I held back. They asked the name of my group, and I said, "Hope: There's Hope in Jesus." Every Wednesday, ten to fifteen residents in wheelchairs wait to hear God's Word, praying for healing and restoration. They have accepted Jesus as their Savior. I gave them "One Billion Souls" T-shirts and encouraged them to share their faith with the other 90 residents, some of whom are facing death and confined to their rooms. I am overwhelmed by God's love and restoration.
>
> One Wednesday evening, I was told the director needed to speak with me. On that Thursday, she offered me a pastoral care position. I hesitated, having just retired, but she insisted I was the right person. She explained that new residents needed assessments and prayers, and this would give me access to the entire facility. Remembering Pastor Tim's sermon about souls being saved through healing, I knew God was opening a door for the "One Billion Souls" assignment. My mentor, Elder Vicky, said, "God will honor your yes." So I said yes. From a cardboard box, God washed my feet so I could wash others' feet. Sitting with a client, I learned that manicures were only available once a month. I decided to find out when, planning to wash their feet and offer them the bread of life: His Word, His promises, His hope to those who don't believe there is hope.

God used several people along the way to bring Maria to Christ. Perhaps your journey with Jesus is the result of many people's faithfulness, prayers, and words as well. Each of us has the opportunity to be part of the "ten" and of many fish stories. The challenge is to remember that you are the "one" in the "one billion starts with one." To each of us, God has given the assignment of making sure we do not go to heaven alone. Let's go deep sea fishing and bring as many people with us as we can.

313 CONVERSATIONS AND CONVERSIONS

I still remember my first cell phone—the Motorola Razor. It was shortly after 2000, and since I lived in Detroit at the time, my area code was 313. Even my kids remember my old phone number, which I kept for years until I recently switched to the classic 212 New York City area code.

Whenever I see that area code 313, I think of something far bigger than Detroit. It is a number that is significant on our road to a billion souls. It is what has been missing: what I call "313 conversations and conversions."

Thomas Aquinas, a thirteenth-century Dominican priest and one of the church's great theologians, explained that "when you want to convert someone, you go over to where he is standing, take him by the hand, and guide him. You don't stand across the room and shout at him. You don't order him to come over where you are. You start where he is and work from that position."[26] It seems that the western church is often shouting at people to come to church on Sunday, forgetting that there is so much more that is involved. After all, why didn't Jesus just distribute His sermon notes to the masses to easily gain more disciples? It is because His greatest words were never from a prepared sermon but simply came during unexpected encounters with people. That's what it was all about.

Jesus spoke some of His most powerful words over dinners or in response to someone's question. Many of the verses that we think are intended for preaching as sermons actually came from personal conversations. Even the most famous evangelistic verse, John 3:16, was spoken during a one-on-one meeting with a Jewish rabbi who was so afraid to be seen with Jesus that he approached Him at night.

Many leaders today have been trained to prepare sermons but not to be prepared for encounters. We have learned how to speak to many people but not to one person. Yet all of the sermons in the book of Acts were extemporaneous. They weren't messages prepared in a study but were spoken in the moment, often unexpectedly. That's why it is not entirely surprising that the following is attributed to the great D. L. Moody: "I have won more people to Christ by holy conversations than all my meetings."

Lately I have been praying for God to give me holy conversations—people to talk to outside of the church. I remember reading an anecdotal story about Moody being in an elevator when a man walked in. Moody immediately said to him, "Sir, do you know if you're going to heaven today?"

The man replied, "Sir, you are either the rudest man I've ever met, or you're D. L. Moody."

Wherever Moody went, he intended to share the gospel. We, too, must be trained for those everyday moments—what I refer to as "313 conversations." Why 313? It is because there are 313 non-Sunday days each year, all the Mondays through Saturdays. While churches around the world spend most of their resources focusing on the 52, I want to be reignited and equipped for the 313—the conversations that happen in our daily lives, Monday through Saturday, outside the church walls.

When I read about Moody's experience in that elevator, I began to pray, "God, give me those elevator conversations." I was in Indianapolis some years ago during NBA season, and I learned that the Houston Rockets were in town playing the Indiana Pacers, and they happened to be staying in the same hotel as me. I prayed to God, "I want an opportunity to share the gospel with the Houston Rockets." I prayed boldly, but I'm not sure I had the courage to speak to them.

My room was on the eighteenth floor, and the team was staying on a special secured level. I don't even know if the elevator had a button for the floor they were on. Yet as I stood at the elevator, waiting to go down, suddenly the doors opened, and there in front of me was the starting lineup of the Houston Rockets! My friend and I walked onto the elevator and I prayed, "I have 18 floors to see the answer. God, give me wisdom!" When the doors closed, I looked at my friend and said, "So, what you're telling me about this Jesus is that if He comes into my life and changes me, I can be a brand-new person? (I was pretending there was an evangelistic conversation already happening before the doors opened up. I was the sinner, and my friend was the evangelist.) I don't have to go to hell? All I have to do is kneel right here in this elevator and say, 'Jesus, come into my life?'" And then I got on my knees in the elevator and said, "Jesus, come in!" Those men were all looking at me, wondering, "What in the world is going on in this elevator?" Just then the doors opened up in the lobby, and I said, "Hallelujah! I'm saved now!" I don't know if they got saved, but they heard the gospel for 18 floors in that elevator. Not only that, the experience changed my life. I saw God directly answer my prayer for help with those 313!

I love to read conversion stories, and it seems the majority of them are the result of 313 conversations. Nicky Cruz didn't just randomly walk into a church one day and get saved. Neither did C. S. Lewis, who got saved on the way to the zoo after considering his many conversations with Christians friends. He tells the story of his conversion in his book *Surprised by Joy: The Shape of My Early Life*.

I recently listened to the interview of a lady named Rosaria Butterfield, whose story is told in *The Secret Thoughts of an Unlikely Convert*. She was a tenured professor at Syracuse University who was deeply involved in LGBTQ activism and was militant toward Christians. She wrote a critical article about evangelicals, and in response, a Reformed Presbyterian minister invited her to dinner. Butterfield said that she was eventually won to Jesus by the hospitality of that pastor. She wouldn't step foot into a church, but she would go to his house, and he would sit down with her every time she walked in. The conversations began to bring her to faith and change her life. She is now married to a pastor, a mother of four, and a powerful mouthpiece for God.[27]

As much as I love all of these conversion stories, I have learned the most about the 313 from people in the Bible like Joseph, Daniel, and Esther. As believers in enemy territory, these three understood it well. Joseph ended up second in charge in Egypt. Daniel was considered to be the prime minister in Persia, and Esther eventually became queen of Persia. Their entire lives were spent "in the elevator." It was as if they had to wear the away jersey all the time. When you walk into your church, you get to put on your home jersey. Everyone is singing the same songs and speaking the same Christian language. If you were to say, "Are you covered by the blood?" people in church would understand. But if you were to say it out on the city streets, you would be arrested. The church has taught people how to act with their home jerseys on but neglected to remind them that most of their lives will be spent as the away team.

Joseph in particular helped give me a grid for navigating my 313 conversations—those times when I'm out of the pulpit, when nobody is shouting "amen" but instead are challenging what I'm saying.

Joseph was thrown into jail after being falsely accused of sexual harassment by his boss's wife. However, it was the opposite that took place. Joseph refused her advancements, and when she didn't get her way, she accused him of rape. Joseph was put in jail by her husband, where he met two men from Pharaoh's court—a baker and a cupbearer. Genesis 40 begins by explaining how the two men had angered Pharaoh, landing them in the same place where Joseph was imprisoned. The captain of the jail put Joseph in charge of them, which of course was the sovereignty of God working everything out. Here is how Joseph responded to them—his "elevator talk":

> When Joseph came to them in the morning and observed them, behold, they were dejected. He asked Pharaoh's officials who were with him in confinement in his master's house, "Why are your faces so sad today?" Then they said to him, "We have had a dream and there is no one to interpret it." Then Joseph said to them, "Do not interpretations belong to God? Tell it to me, please." (Genesis 40:6–8 NASB)

Within just these few verses, there are three things that have helped guide my 313 conversations over the years.

1. OBSERVE PEOPLE

First, it says that Joseph "observed them." He noticed the men and perceived a sadness about them. The other day as Cindy and I were walking back to our apartment, we saw an older man who was having trouble walking. He would go a few steps and then lean on a brick wall. My wife noticed and said, "Let's see if he needs water. We need to check if he needs help." It all starts with simply noticing the people around you. Notice people, their moods, the anger, the tears.

Jesus said in John 4:35, "Behold, I say to you, lift up your eyes, and look on the fields, that they are white for harvest" (NASB). White is the color of grain that is ready to be plucked. It reminds us that there are people all around us who just need someone to notice them. Many times I have witnessed those emotions in people and knew it signaled harvest time. They are usually people who have searched in every other place only to come to a dead end. You don't have to look far these days to see those emotions. According to the National Institute of Mental Health, approximately 59.3 million adults in the United States, which is almost one in four people you encounter, experienced a mental illness in the past year.[28] All around us are people who are facing difficult mental health struggles from anxiety to depression to substance abuse. You can see it in their faces if you simply open up your eyes, and when you see it, you can speak words of hope to them.

You never know how great an impact you can have simply by observing the people around you. I read an amazing story about an 80-year-old couple who began to notice a young man in their apartment building. They were the landlords, and this young man was an entrepreneur who had seemingly done it all—from serving as college president to the work he did in his state. Every time they saw him, the couple would invite him to church. In fact, they invited him so often that he usually tried to avoid them.

The ambitious young man spent nearly every moment investing in his new company, the California Confection Company. He only took time to rest on Sundays, when he would go horseback riding and host a radio show in Hollywood.

Time passed, and after horseback riding one Sunday, he finally decided to go to the couple's church. He went in and sat in the back. He didn't get saved, but he listened. The couple saw him in church and gave his name to the young adult director, who invited him to a gathering. Shortly after, the young man knelt beside his bed and asked Christ to come into his heart.

He eventually left his confection company and started another company. It is estimated that his new company has reached 2 billion people with the gospel. They also created *The Jesus Film*, which has been viewed by over 5 billion people, and has seen over 679 million people come to Christ.[29] This young man—Bill Bright—got saved, and Campus Crusade was birthed, all because an 80-year-old couple observed that no matter how successful he appeared on the outside, he was empty inside. They noticed him and were relentless in their pursuit of him. Start observing people. You have no idea what incredible things God has intended for someone's life!

2. ASK QUESTIONS

The second thing that Joseph did, which we often neglect, is that he simply asked questions. He looked at the baker and cupbearer and asked, "Why are you sad? What's going on?"

After observing people, start asking questions. It can be any question. *How's your day going? How long have you been doing this?* I heard one person say it like this: "He who asks the questions controls the conversation." It is my secret in counseling as well as in evangelism: I constantly ask people questions because I know if I can get them speaking, I will hear what is in their heart. So many people miss it because they want to do all the talking. But when you let the other person speak, you will soon discover the truth of the verse: "Out of the abundance of the heart the mouth speaks" (Matthew 12:34 NASB). Though people may think they can hide what is in their heart, the Bible says that no man has tamed the tongue. In about 20 minutes, I can get that untamed tongue to speak and that heart revealed. Asking people questions not only allows you to hear others' hearts, it also lets them know you care.

I once read the story about how a profound question posed by a dying woman in a hospital room in North Carolina completely changed the course of a young doctor's life:

An eager young doctor with a bright future evaluated his elderly patient with not much future left at all. She had a terminal heart condition that was inoperable. All he could do was treat her symptoms and pain. As the physician visited the dying woman during his daily rounds, they gradually got to know one another. During one particularly poignant conversation, he learned that the woman was a deeply devout Christian. As a confident atheist, he assumed that as her condition deteriorated, her faith would do the same as she realized her God was not coming to the rescue. Yet with every passing day, his patient's faith seemed to grow stronger even as her body weakened.

The doctor found his patient's religious beliefs antiquated but charming. But then, he was taken aback by her forthright inquiry: "Doctor, I have been telling you what I believe, but what do you believe?"

He was a bit shaken by her question. He murmured something about the beauty of the natural world and left the conversation with a degree of unease. He was one of the best trained scientists of his generation. By his own reckoning, there was no one who better understood the systems and laws that keep nature running. But he was deeply unsettled by the way the dying woman slept peacefully in her hospital bed while he lay awake each night, haunted by her question. How could she be so confident of her view of the world and her place in it? Shouldn't she, at death's doorstep, be the sleepless one? He became convinced that his inability to answer her question or find consolation in his view of the mechanical universe was intellectually unacceptable.

Over the next two years, the young physician read voraciously about Buddhism, Christianity, Hinduism, Islam, and Judaism, examining the data about their roots and claims, seeking to find one that would help him satisfactorily answer the dying woman's question. Ultimately, while hiking in Oregon's Cascade Mountains, he came to the conclusion that the claims of Christianity best explained what he saw around him. He began to embrace the faith of his former patient, who had begun a kind of "cascade" within him with her one honest question.[30]

This is the story of Francis Collins, one of the most respected scientists of our day. He is a physician and geneticist known for key breakthroughs in identifying disease genes as well as leading the Human Genome Project. He served as director of the National Institutes of Health, appointed by President Obama and reappointed by President Trump. Because of his leadership roles, when Collins became a Christian, it impacted not only his life but the lives of many others as well. And to think—a single question from a dying Christian was the catalyst for one of the greatest scientists of our generation to become born again. It didn't happen in a church. It was a 313 conversation!

3. THE GOD PART

We observe, we ask questions, and then comes the God part. Joseph did not start with God. In fact, God does not even come into the conversation until after his observations and questions. Finally, Joseph said regarding their dreams, "Don't interpretations belong to God?"

My favorite convert in the actual 313 Detroit area happened the night before I was leaving to move to New York. He was an older Korean man named Hung, and he was my dry cleaners for ten years. After preaching 3,000 sermons over my 30 years in Detroit, on a Tuesday night in July, I gave an altar call, and Hung walked the aisle to be born again. It wasn't until after ten years of noticing him week after week, asking questions about what he believes, ordering "shirts, no starch and on hangers" and spending a lot of money on dry cleaning!

As we step out in faith, God is always faithful to do His part. I encourage you to begin praying for Him to give you those 313 conversations and conversions. Start by observing those around you and taking the time to ask questions. It won't be long before you find yourself engaged in 313 conversations, with God doing His part—transforming lives. After all, who would have imagined that simply starting a conversation would bring someone like Rosaria Butterfield or Francis Collins to Christ? You never know who you are speaking to or how many lives will be impacted for the kingdom of God!

07

GOING 100 MILES OUT OF THE WAY TO CHANGE THE WORLD

Not long ago, I was riding the elevator in my apartment building with a gentleman who lives on our floor. I've known him for a while—he's single, a friendly young man who works in finance. We have chatted a little in the past, and he knows that I am a pastor. As we were in the elevator, he mentioned he was on his way to a very important presentation with his financial partners. I was headed to an appointment myself, so we quickly parted ways. Yet as I thought back on what seemed to be a casual elevator conversation, I suddenly sensed in my spirit that I had missed an opportunity.

I felt the Holy Spirit say, "You should have prayed for him." I repented and told God I would pray now and apologize the next time I saw him. Days went by, and I didn't run into him. With each passing day, the thought of apologizing seemed more and more awkward. However, when I eventually saw him, I explained, "When you told me you had an important meeting, I was supposed to pray for you, and I missed it. Please forgive me. Once we left, I prayed that God would help you."

He was very kind and said, "Tim, it went so well, and it's probably because you did pray for me when you left there."

That's all there is to the story. There isn't even a punchline. That's it for now, though I believe something bigger was supposed to happen. I had my mind focused on my appointment and was in such a rush that I bypassed a very important conversation—one that was interrupting my plans.

This chapter is about something that God has deeply impressed upon my heart. If we can lay hold of it, I believe we can change the world. It's about going a hundred miles out of the way for the sake of one person. One of my spiritual fathers, Leonard Ravenhill, once said: "We believe to the point of inconvenience."[31] However, we must understand that those seemingly inconvenient conversations can have an eternal impact. The apostle Paul put it this way: We are to be "ready in season and out of season."

> Rise to the occasion and preach when it is convenient and when it is not. (2 Timothy 4:2 TPT)

When I am in the pulpit, we can call it "in season." I have prepared and prayed for the message. But the out-of-season challenge comes during those spontaneous conversations, often occurring at the most inconvenient moments. When our plans and appointments are being interrupted, it is easy to miss the voice of the Holy Spirit, just like I did. The Lord may simply be telling you to pray for someone. It is much easier when it is a planned meeting, and you can ask God beforehand to help you prepare. But when you have to catch a cab, make a train, or get to a meeting, it's easy to miss His still, small voice.

Acts 8 tells the story of someone who didn't miss his opportunity, despite the inconvenience. What I love about this chapter is how clearly it shows that one billion starts with one. It all began when God interrupted a revival service so that one person could hear the gospel.

To set the scene, Stephen, the first martyr, was just stoned to death at the end of the previous chapter. Acts 8 opens with Christian families being dragged from their homes by a madman named Saul. Of course, only God could take a man like that and transform him into the apostle Paul! In the midst of persecution, God was still moving.

> Therefore, those who had been scattered went about preaching the word. And Philip went down to the city of Samaria and began proclaiming Christ to them. (Acts 8:4–5 NASB)

At first glance, there seems to be a lot wrong with this verse, though everything is right with it in God's eyes. From a human perspective, the when, where, and who are all wrong. That's what makes this story nothing but miraculous. God used persecution, a waiter, and an outcast people to bring the first revival outside of Jerusalem!

The intense persecution actually helped speed up this revival. Imagine preaching and constantly looking over your shoulder to see if the government is going to come in and shut things down. The closest I came to that was when I was preaching in a church in a very militant Muslim area of Bangladesh. I had to whisper the entire message!

Now the waiter was Philip from Acts 6. He had no training and was working in a soup kitchen for widows. But Philip was full of the Spirit. We have no record of him ever preaching, yet God sends him to help catalyze revival among the Samaritans—an outcast people hated by the Jews. The Samaritans were half Jewish and half Assyrian, so the Jews considered them impure. Then God made things even worse on the "who" part. Not only did He use a waiter, but He sent two men from Jerusalem to help Philip pray for people to receive the Holy Spirit. One of those men was someone with an interesting past. Look at what this man had prayed just two years prior for these people:

> And He sent messengers on ahead of Him. And they went, and entered a village of the Samaritans, to make arrangements for Him. And they did not receive Him, because He was journeying with His face toward Jerusalem. And when His disciples James and John saw this, they said, "Lord, do You want us to command fire to come down from heaven and consume them?" But He turned and rebuked them, and said, "You do not know what kind of spirit you are of; for the Son of Man did not come to destroy men's lives, but to save them." (Luke 9:52–56 NASB)

James and John were offering, "Lord, they didn't treat you very well. Would you like us to pray one of those 'kill you' prayers?" Two years later, look who is coming to help in Samaria.

> Now when the apostles in Jerusalem heard that Samaria had received the word of God, they sent them Peter and John, who came down and prayed for them, that they might receive the Holy Spirit. (Acts 8:14–15 NASB)

This is the same John from Luke 9 who wanted to burn them up! He got the fire wrong; he was going to pray fire to kill them when God wanted the fire of the Holy Spirit to fill them.

So now you have a bona fide revival among the most unlikely group of people, with the help of two of the most unexpected of individuals—one who is completely unqualified to preach, and the other who could be considered a former racist. But God says, "Those are the ones I have chosen to use." Large crowds gather, signs and wonders follow, demons are cast out, and the city rejoices. Even the town's occult leader is converted. Countless numbers of men and women are getting saved and baptized. They send in the big guns, the apostles, to come and participate. Another Pentecostal outpouring is happening, not in Jerusalem, but in Samaria!

Here comes the part I want you to notice. While the city is experiencing revival and rejoicing, God suddenly interrupts Philip for an "out-of-season" moment—one that would change the world. The problem was that it was completely out of the way, a huge inconvenience for Philip.

> So, when they had solemnly testified and spoken the word of the Lord, they started back to Jerusalem, and were preaching the gospel to many villages of the Samaritans. But an angel of the Lord spoke to Philip saying, "Get up and go south to the road that descends from Jerusalem to Gaza." (Acts 8:25–26 NASB)

This is a desert road. The journey from Samaria to Gaza would have been roughly a hundred miles—a huge inconvenience, particularly when you are in the middle of these wonderful church services. People are getting saved and filled with the Holy Spirit. Yet God leaves Peter and John in charge and sends Philip elsewhere. I would have asked, "Why, who, where?" But Philip is simply told to go with no further details.

God was about to use Philip in a way he never expected, but it required him going out of his way. He had to be willing to be inconvenienced. We should all have "Philip stories" of divine guidance. This is my challenge to you; this is where one billion starts with one. It happens with what I call the nudge, the talk, and the possibility.

1. THE NUDGE

It all starts with the nudge of the Holy Spirit. The nudge often comes out of season, and it calls for obedience on our part, no matter how inconvenient. I felt that nudge a couple of weeks ago during the 10 a.m. service. I was sitting where I normally sit, perfectly at peace, having a great worship time with the Lord, when

God suddenly interrupted me. He told me to go pray for an elder who had been experiencing pain. That meant I would have to walk in front of everybody right in the middle of worship. After briefly insisting that I could pray for him later, I decided I knew better. I got up, walked over to the elder and prayed for him. I later received this email from him:

> Jesus touched me! Pastor Tim, I have not felt a single pain stab since Sunday, May 4th, when you came over to pray for me. Up to that point, the sudden pain in my shoulder was 3–4 times every day, and the intensity was increasing. I had been to the surgeon a few weeks back, and X-rays showed my torn rotator and dislocating shoulder joint. The doctor said I would have to endure the pain of PT in order to strengthen the tendons and muscles in hopes of avoiding shoulder replacement. I had started PT, and the surgeon was right—the pain was crazy . . . until May 4th! I have since been in four sessions pain-free and mobility is increasing. The PT doctor is amazed!

We know this is the power of Jesus Christ, and it all started with a nudge!

It was a nudge I felt when we went to Liberty University for my daughter's graduation. We were checking out of the hotel, and we were speaking with a precious woman who had been so kind to us. She was a Muslim woman, and I felt the nudge of the Holy Spirit saying, "Pray for her."

I looked her and asked, "Can I pray for you?"

She said, "I'm Muslim."

"Great, let me pray for you." I prayed for her, and as we were walking out, my daughter said, "Did you see her? She was weeping while we were praying for her!"

I once heard a statement from an older man, which I have reframed slightly: "You can never experience the continual nudge of the Holy Ghost if you cannot say this statement: 'Lord, I'm willing to do whatever You want me to do, no matter what the cost.'" If you can't say that, you won't feel the nudge because you will be embarrassed, inconvenienced, and interrupted by God. He doesn't care what is scheduled on your calendar when somebody needs to be prayed for or needs to hear the gospel. He will even interrupt a revival service like he did with Philip.

> Now an angel of the Lord spoke to Philip, saying, "Arise and go toward the south along the road which goes down from Jerusalem to Gaza." This is desert. So he arose and went. (Acts 8:26–27 NKJV)

I love that when the angel of the Lord told Philip to arise and go, he simply arose and went!

> And behold, a man of Ethiopia, a eunuch of great authority under Candace the queen of the Ethiopians, who had charge of all her treasury, and had come to Jerusalem to worship, was returning. And sitting in his chariot, he was reading Isaiah the prophet. Then the Spirit said to Philip, "Go near and overtake this chariot." (Acts 8:27–29 NKJV)

Whenever you get up and go to do what God wants you to do, get ready to behold. Look for something that makes you exclaim, "Wow, I never would have experienced this if I hadn't gotten up and gone!" You cannot behold the potential miracle without a desert road obedience, which often comes without an explanation. Who would've thought that a little nudge would lead Philip to Ethiopia?

One Sunday, as Dr. Teresa Conlon was preaching, I felt a nudge from the Holy Spirit saying, "End the service with joy." I quickly texted our worship leader to get ready. After the message, we had Mama May, who has been with the choir for decades, and Elder Vicki lead the congregation in singing the old Andre Crouch song, "Can't Nobody Do Me Like Jesus." That day happened to be Mama May's 80th birthday, and there she was on stage, singing and dancing her heart out. I received a text from Mama May the following Monday:

> Hello my dear pastor! I had a wonderful birthday yesterday! First Ricardo and the choir sang happy birthday before the service, then you announced it was my birthday, age 80 years, then the choir had a big birthday cake at lunch time. But my big surprise is when bro Kareem called me to sing. I enjoyed it.
>
> When I was leaving the church, a young lady told me she was watching the service online, and when she saw the lady in white came out and was dancing, she put on some clothes and came to the church. She lives two blocks away. She stayed for the 1 p.m. service and she went down to the altar to be saved. That made my day. She did not even recognize me when we were talking because I had my coat on and a hat on my head. Best birthday I ever had.

It started with that nudge to end the service with joy. Who knew that a young lady would be watching online, see the rejoicing on stage, run two blocks to get to church, and then get saved? When you obey, get ready to behold what God can do!

2. THE CONVERSATION

Then comes the second part: the conversation. That's the faith part. "Go up and join the chariot." Philip could have come up with a myriad of excuses. *I'm not the right person for this. He's an Ethiopian; I'm Jewish. He's rich; I'm poor.* Nevertheless, Philip went up by faith.

> Philip ran up and heard him reading Isaiah the prophet, and said, "Do you understand what you are reading?" And he said, "Well, how could I, unless someone guides me?" And he invited Philip to come up and sit with him. Now the passage of Scripture which he was reading was this:
>
> "HE WAS LED AS A SHEEP TO SLAUGHTER; AND AS A LAMB BEFORE ITS SHEARER IS SILENT, SO HE DOES NOT OPEN HIS MOUTH. IN HUMILIATION HIS JUDGMENT WAS TAKEN AWAY; WHO WILL RELATE HIS GENERATION? FOR HIS LIFE IS REMOVED FROM THE EARTH." (Acts 8:30–33 NASB)

Cindy and I were in Boston last year for just 24 hours, and a friend of mine had recommended that I visit a certain place—a wall of a building. There isn't even a store that exists there; it is simply a plaque on a cement wall. It took us a while to find it. The story behind the plaque involves the faith of a church volunteer named Edward Kimball. He taught a teenage Sunday school class and noticed there was a young man who would just fall asleep, showing no interest in what was happening. Yet Kimball felt the nudge of the Holy Spirit. The teenager worked at a shoe store, so Kimball came to meet Dwight during his lunch break. This was the faith step—having a conversation with this young man who didn't have any interest in God. But that conversation led to the young man's salvation. And now the plaque in Boston reads:

> D. L. Moody
> Christian evangelist,
> Friend of man,
> Founder of the Northfield Schools,
> was converted to God in a shoe store on this site.
> April 21, 1855

Dwight Lyman Moody was one of the greatest American evangelists of the nineteenth century. He had such an incredible impact for the kingdom of God, but one of my favorite stories is when he preached at Cambridge in England, where a young athlete named C.T. Studd happened to be in the audience. He was a star cricketer, a man of great ability and also of great wealth. His father was a multimillionaire and personal friend to the queen. Studd had it all. But when he heard Moody preach, God touched his life. To his family's dismay, Studd resigned from school and all athletics. He was part of a group of seven young men who got saved at Cambridge and felt God calling them to bring the gospel to China. They went, met up with Hudson Taylor, and what took place is absolutely historic.[32] According to church historian Leonard Sweet, China is now on track to have more Christians than the entire population of the United States. In a country where Christianity is illegal, there are 300 million Christians.[33] It all goes back to the faith of one Sunday school teacher to have a conversation with a shoe clerk!

In faith, Philip jumped up on the chariot and asked, "Do you understand what you are reading?" (Acts 8:30). He simply opened with a question. There are some questions I often ask people to help open up gospel conversations. For example:

If you were to die today, do you know if you're going to heaven?

I believe in God, so I believe in miracles. Is there anything I can pray with you about?

Has anyone ever told you that God loves you?

Life is so fragile. What do you think happens to us after we die?

A couple of weeks ago, Cindy and I were sitting with dear friends, Dr. O. S. and Susie Hawkins, at the Brooklyn Diner. We sat there for three hours, just talking about the things of the Lord. As we were sharing a piece of cheesecake and getting ready to wrap things up, O. S. started a conversation with our waiter, who we will call Johnny. He was from West Africa. O. S. asked him, "Johnny, do you know that you're going to heaven?"

Johnny replied, "Eighty percent."

I've never heard this answer before. He went on to explain, "I'm a Muslim. I'm hoping that all the works I've done will be pleasing to God so I can get to heaven."

With my lack of faith, I was thinking, "Oh, he's a Muslim. Let's just pray and go." But O. S. wouldn't let it go. He said, "Let me tell you something. Your good works can't get you there. You're trying to get there by do, do, do, do. And I'm here to tell you it's been done, done, done, done. Jesus died for your sins. He died so you could be saved."

Johnny says, "Tell me more." So O. S. shares with him how to be born again. All of a sudden he asks, "Would you like to pray for Christ to come in and change you?"

"Absolutely," Johnny replies. Right there in the diner, he prayed for Jesus to come into his heart. We brought a Bible the next day for Johnny and invited him to church. Even though I had my doubts, thankfully with God, all things are possible! We hear the word "Muslim" or we hear someone say, "I'm not interested" and we immediately back off. But O. S. just took a step of faith and started a conversation.

3. THE POSSIBILITY

When you combine obedience and faith, you never know what miracle will take place! That's why I apologized to my neighbor after our elevator conversation. I never want to miss what God is saying. I never want to miss the out-of-season moment. I want the Lord to trust me just like He did Philip, leading him on a desert road to meet the CFO of Ethiopia.

> Then Philip opened his mouth, and beginning from this Scripture he preached Jesus to him. As they went along the road they came to some water; and the eunuch said, "Look! Water! What prevents me from being baptized?" And Philip said, "If you believe with all your heart, you may." And he answered and said, "I believe that Jesus Christ is the Son of God." And he ordered the chariot to stop; and they both went down into the water, Philip as well as the eunuch, and he baptized him. (Acts 8:35–38 NASB)

Philip probably thought it was just a conversation, but it ended with a salvation and water baptism! Yet what happened that day had far greater ramifications than just one eunuch getting saved. I want to give you proof that one billion starts with one. A continent was changed because of a conversation.

It is confirmed by Bible historians and even an editorial in *The Wall Street Journal* that the entrance of the gospel of Jesus into the continent of Africa was by this Ethiopian eunuch.[34] One conversation, and the gospel enters Ethiopia. Today there are 54 different countries in that continent and approximately 1.5 billion people.[35] Let's just take the last hundred years. In 1900, there were 10 million Christians. By 1950, there were over 50 million Christians. In 2000, there were 400 million Christians. The latest statistic in 2024 tells us that there are 734 million Christians in Africa![36] That's about three quarters of a billion Christians—all from one conversation!

Remember, you don't get Africa if you don't obey the nudge, go down a desert road, and have a conversation by faith. There are people who have yet to be saved all around the world because we haven't had the out-of-season conversations. The church today has largely become barren, forgetting that we have been born again to reproduce.

What kind of people change the world? Those who will move on a nudge. It's the people who are willing to have their plans interrupted and step out in faith. I hope you are convinced that one billion truly does start with one. It's one conversation. Open up your mouth—not just in church, but out there where people need to hear the gospel. Philip took his opportunity and began to proclaim Jesus, and we are called to do the same. There may be a family, an apartment building, a dorm, a business group, or even a continent at stake. Respond to the nudge, have a conversation, and then leave the possibility up to a God who does the miraculous!

08

CAN MY PRAYER LIFE OPEN UP PRISON DOORS?

I am fully convinced that a praying church is the key to a billion souls. That's why there is an urgency in my heart to sound the trumpet for the church to fight on her knees once again. Even Isaiah the prophet cried out with these words:

> No one turns to you in prayer; no one goes to you for help. You have hidden yourself from us and have abandoned us because of our sins. (Isaiah 64:7 GNT)

Isaiah was pleading, "Is there a praying person in the house? Is there a praying church in your country? A praying small group willing to believe God?" Without people praying, sin takes over, and God hides His face. Prayer is what stands between a nation and the chaos of sin. When the church chooses to pray, the miraculous occurs.

Acts 12 illustrates this well with a story about a prison cell and a prayer meeting. An incredible deliverance occurred the night before an apostle's scheduled execution—all because a house prayer meeting rewrote the story.

> Now about that time Herod the king laid hands on some who belonged to the church, in order to mistreat them. And he had James the brother of John put to death with a sword. And when he saw that it pleased the Jews, he

proceeded to arrest Peter also. Now it was during the days of Unleavened Bread. And when he had seized him, he put him in prison, delivering him to four squads of soldiers to guard him, intending after the Passover to bring him out before the people. So Peter was kept in the prison, but prayer for him was being made fervently by the church to God.

And on the very night when Herod was about to bring him forward, Peter was sleeping between two soldiers, bound with two chains; and guards in front of the door were watching over the prison. And behold, an angel of the Lord suddenly appeared, and a light shone in the cell; and he struck Peter's side and roused him, saying, "Get up quickly." And his chains fell off his hands. And the angel said to him, "Gird yourself and put on your sandals." And he did so. And he said to him, "Wrap your cloak around you and follow me." And he went out and continued to follow, and he did not know that what was being done by the angel was real, but thought he was seeing a vision. And when they had passed the first and second guard, they came to the iron gate that leads into the city, which opened for them by itself; and they went out and went along one street; and immediately the angel departed from him. And when Peter came to himself, he said, "Now I know for sure that the Lord has sent forth His angel and rescued me from the hand of Herod and from all that the Jewish people were expecting." And when he realized this, he went to the house of Mary, the mother of John who was also called Mark, where many were gathered together and were praying. And when he knocked at the door of the gate, a servant-girl named Rhoda came to answer. And when she recognized Peter's voice, because of her joy she

> did not open the gate, but ran in and announced that Peter was standing in front of the gate. And they said to her, "You are out of your mind!" But she kept insisting that it was so. And they kept saying, "It is his angel." But Peter continued knocking; and when they had opened the door, they saw him and were amazed. But motioning to them with his hand to be silent, he described to them how the Lord had led him out of the prison. (Acts 12:1–17 NASB)

It was this very passage of scripture that sparked a heated discussion between my professor and me back when I was doing graduate work at a seminary. The debate was over the power of prayer and God's sovereignty. My professor's theology led him to believe that we pray because we are commanded to, not because prayer brings about change. I had to pause and ask him a couple of times, "Why do we pray?" His answer remained the same: "We pray because the Bible says to. Peter's release was simply up to the sovereignty of God." At that point, I couldn't stay silent any longer. I wasn't dismissing his statement, yet he left out a critical thing—the fact that a prayer meeting was taking place across town for Peter's release.

I asked my professor, "In light of the prayer meeting and the content of their prayers, could the story be teaching us something on the power of prayer? Is it possible that God intentionally included the story of the prayer meeting so that we would connect the two things—prayer and freedom from captivity?" I continued to explain my reasoning: "It's interesting that James is killed by Herod, but Peter is delivered by an angel. It just seems that the difference between these two was a prayer meeting. Could it be that God is challenging us to pray for prison doors to open and for people to be set free?"

My final question to the professor was this: "If the church hadn't prayed, would Peter have been set free?"

As we consider this question, let's look again at the verse in Acts:

> So Peter was kept in the prison, but prayer for him was being made fervently by the church to God. (Acts 12:5 NASB)

I believe those four little words altered the outcome of Peter's story: "But prayer for him . . ."

What if someone's life depended on your prayer life?

It's a challenging thought. Lately I have been asking myself the question: *Can my prayer life open up prison doors?* There have been times when I have been so busy that I have neglected to pray. It makes me wonder if there are people in bondage because I didn't intercede. Are there healings and salvations that needed prayer? Are there prayerless prisons holding people captive simply because no one prayed?

"Men who prayed most accomplished most" is attributed to Dr. Leonard Ravenhill, one of my spiritual mentors. I have seen this hold true countless times over the years. In fact, I just received an email from one of our online leaders, Brian, demonstrating the power of prayer:

> I called a woman today to lead her in prayer prior to her scheduled water baptism in the morning on Zoom, after first service. Here is what I found out:
>
> Michele in Florida has been watching for two years online. In April this year, in the middle of service, you prayed for healing for the congregation.
>
> Michele was suffering from stage 4 liver disease, along with a rare form of diabetes, a terminal illness. When you led the prayer for healing, she got down on her knees and anointed herself with olive oil, praying along with you for

> God to heal her. She said she felt something change.
>
> Yesterday, 5/23, she received her lab report back with a note from the doctor. "Great news, your lab work came back perfect! No liver disease, no diabetes."
>
> Today 5/24 is her birthday and she is celebrating it, rejoicing in her lab results and God's answered prayer. Tomorrow on 5/25, she is excited to experience water baptism, likely in a kiddie pool, as part of the TSC online family! What an incredible weekend for her, praise God!

When you decide to pray, you never know who might be saved, delivered, healed, or set free!

Remember, it was Herod who imprisoned both James and Peter. Two people in prison, held by the same person for the same thing. James was put death by the sword, and we know for sure that Herod intended to kill Peter as well. It is no accident that the Holy Spirit included in the Scriptures that a prayer meeting was happening for Peter's deliverance. I believe God is saying, "I want you to see what can happen when the church begins to pray!" On the eve of Peter's death, prayer was being made fervently by the church, and prayer ultimately trumped Herod's evil intentions!

The word "fervent" here stands out to me. I'm reminded of what it says in James 5:16: "The effectual fervent prayer of a righteous man availeth much" (KJV). That word "fervent" means "to stretch out." It was a description of a runner approaching the finish line, stretching to win. One dictionary even links the word to a torture rack that would stretch an individual, bringing their limbs to the breaking point. It reminds us that miracles happen when the church is willing to be stretched in prayer. Here are just some of the results of fervent prayer:

Fervent prayer can overcome evil intentions of others. No matter what is being plotted against us, prayer invites God's intervention and protection.

Fervent prayer can open up prison doors and break off chains. It can set free those who are locked in addictions, unhealthy mindsets, and depression.

Fervent prayer can be contagious, igniting the church to pray again. This kind of prayer awakens something in the hearts of those who hear it. I believe God is reigniting passion for prayer among His people.

Fervent prayer meetings can call even young people into the ministry. Do you realize who was in that prayer meeting and saw Peter miraculously released?

> And when he realized this, he went to the house of Mary, the mother of John who was also called Mark, where many were gathered together and were praying. (Acts 12:12 NASB)

At the end of that chapter, we see Mark again, along with Barnabas and Paul.

> And Barnabas and Saul returned from Jerusalem when they had fulfilled their mission, taking along with them John, who was also called Mark. (Acts 12:25 NASB)

The kid at the prayer meeting would eventually be the third member of the team going out on the very first missionary journey! Who knows who might get called when the church begins to pray!

While it's clear that God is calling His church back to prayer, my heart has been grieved by what I see happening in much of the church across our nation. Pastors are playing secular music as they ride around on a rollercoaster on stage. Others are riding in on cyber trucks, getting haircuts and manicures during the sermon. This is what Thomas Bergler, author of *The Juvenilization of American Christianity*, calls the "adolescent church." It is churches today taking on patterns of adolescent teens. Bergler points out that church services are losing something as they begin to spiral downward into resembling a children's church. He explained that adolescents try to be different but all end up looking the same. They all have the same hair, the same clothes, and the same shoes.[37] I witnessed this when I was in Newark Airport, boarding an early flight. I watched 15 adolescent young ladies get on the plane, all trying to be different yet all looking the same. They were all wearing Uggs, sweats, had the same hairstyle, and carried a pillow and a blanket. Then they all sat down and got on their phones. Right after them came a whole group of Hasidic Jews, all looking exactly the same, yet ironically appearing more normal than the teens.

Bergler explained that when someone turns 13 and begins adolescence, they start changing biologically and mentally. They become self-conscious, and their focus shifts to relationships, attaining status among their peers, and feeling good about themselves. The author draws a parallel between these characteristics of adolescents and the church today.[38] They don't even call it a church service but a "worship experience." High-budget stage entertainment has replaced prayer and the presence of God. If the presence of God is not there, we resort to a circus in our churches. If only the church would pray, the circus would stop.

In Matthew 9, Jesus tells us exactly what these last days will require: intercessors and laborers.

> And seeing the multitudes, He felt compassion for them, because they were distressed and downcast like sheep without a shepherd. Then He said to His disciples, "The

> harvest is plentiful, but the workers are few. Therefore beseech the Lord of the harvest to send out workers into His harvest." (Matthew 9:36–38 NASB)

"Beseech" is a fervency word. Jesus is telling us that we need to pray and that we need workers. Sadly, prayer is a weapon that has largely been put away. Ministries and denominations would rather come up with formulas and manuals instead of calling a prayer meeting. It is time to heed what Billy Graham once said: "To get nations back on their feet, we must first get the church down on its knees."[39]

A. W. Tozer put it this way: "To desire revival and at the same time to neglect prayer and devotion is to wish one way and walk another."[40] If we are believing God for a billion souls, we must understand that it all starts with a life of prayer. The power of prayer is directly connected to the end-time harvest of souls. This was clearly evidenced in what was called the Hebrides Revival, which took place from 1949 through 1953. Off the west coast of Scotland is a small group of islands called the Hebrides, and that is where two elderly sisters, Peggy and Christine Smith, began to pray. One was 84 and blind, and the other was 82 and crippled. They decided to start a prayer meeting because they realized that no young people were attending the church. The two ladies began to pray twice a week on Tuesdays and Fridays. They got on their knees at 10 p.m. and would remain on their knees until 3 a.m., believing for revival to take place.

Peggy, the one who was crippled, soon had a vision that the church would be crowded with young people. They persuaded their minister and seven deacons to meet them in prayer. Then one night in November, a young man began to pray with them and started to cry out, "God, are my hands clean? Is my heart pure?" He got no further when they all fell to the ground, asking God to cleanse them. Within a matter of minutes, three elders also fell down. The minister and other intercessors were gripped by conviction and realized that holiness and godliness were what God was demanding of them. They eventually called a young man named Duncan Campbell to hold a series of meetings. On December 13, 1949, at the end of the meeting, all had left. It was just a small meeting. Yet the deacon said to Duncan Campbell, "Don't be discouraged. God is hovering over us. He'll break through. I hear the rumbling of heaven's chariot wheels!"

Duncan Campbell began to pray and then fell into a trance. Five minutes later, he learned that five young people had given their heart to God. He was happy but knew it wasn't enough. He continued to pray when all of a sudden, the man came back and said, "Mr. Campbell, something wonderful has happened! We were praying that God would pour out water on our islands. He's done it. Will you come to the door?"

It was now eleven o'clock at night, and they looked outside the door to find around 700 people gathered there! They were moved by a power they could not explain. A hunger gripped them, and that meeting continued until 4 a.m.! As young people started to run to the church, others who had gone to bed were awakened by the Holy Spirit, got dressed, and felt they were supposed to go to church. Over the next few nights, hundreds gathered in different places, churches, barns, and fields. There were prayer meetings at noon. People would stop and pray for hours, and it continued until thousands and thousands of people came to Christ![41]

During my early years of ministry, I had a friend with a sign posted on his door that I saw every day: "We have to *pray* the price." It is costly, but when we pray, God moves. I love the words of David in Psalm 56:9: "The very day I call for help, the tide of battle turns. My enemies flee! This one thing I know: God is for me!" (TLB). This is praying in battle times. It is two 80-year-old women who saw a battle for their island and chose to pray. It is the early church seeing a battle for Peter's life and turning the tide through prayer.

To have the weapon of prayer yet fail to use it reminds me of a study that I once did in the book of Judges. There was a tribe called Ephraim that did not get called to fight in the battles that the Israelites faced. Neither Jephthah nor Gideon called upon them.

Then the men of Ephraim were summoned, and they crossed to Zaphon and said to Jephthah, "Why did you cross over to fight against the sons of Ammon without calling us to go with you?" (Judges 12:1 NASB)

Then the men of Ephraim said to him, "What is this thing you have done to us, not calling us when you went to fight against Midian?" (Judges 8:1 NASB)

No one called on them because Ephraim had a reputation:

> The sons of Ephraim were archers equipped with bows, yet they turned back in the day of battle. (Psalm 78:9 NASB)

They were archers equipped with bows, yet they never took a shot! Prayer is a weapon. It's an arrow that is shot into heaven. We have the weapon that can turn the tide of the battle, but how often do we fail to use it? How many unshot arrows do we have? Every morning, God says, "Take a shot. There's a battle waging!" When we use our weapon of prayer, we see God move in ways that we never could have fathomed.

Just recently, Times Square Church was in the *New York Post* in an article titled "Andrew Lloyd Webber Dreams of Buying the famous Theater, the Best Stage on Broadway."

> In America, Andrew Lloyd Webber is best known as the composer of "The Phantom of the Opera," "Evita,"

"Cats" and "Sunset Boulevard," among many other popular musicals.

But in London, the Brit also has a reputation as a major West End theater owner . . . .

But there's one building on Broadway he's had his eye on for years—the Mark Hellinger Theatre on West 51st Street.

Never heard of it?

That's because today the 1600-seat house where "My Fair Lady" and Lloyd Webber's "Jesus Christ Superstar" long ago premiered is the Times Square Church, an interdenominational place of worship adjacent to "Wicked." And it's one of the neighborhood's most desirable pieces of real estate.

"It has the best stage on Broadway," Lloyd Webber exclusively told The Post during a sit-down. "It was the premier house, really, for musicals," he added. "Everybody's tried [to buy it]."

. . . The Nederlander Organization first leased the [Hellinger] to the Times Square Church in 1989 — when the neighborhood was dirty and dangerous and the theater business was wobbly — for five years at $1 million a year.

In 1991, the church bought the Hellinger for $17 million. With a congregation of more than 8,000 who regularly fill the collection plate, it's now worth several times that . . . .

Other power players who've tried to snap up the old Hellinger include British producer Cameron Mackintosh and crooked Canadian showman Garth Drabinsky. But everybody who's gone up against God has given up.

> "That pastor there," Lloyd Webber said of senior pastor Tim Dilena, "he's just got one organ, a little stage, him and a microphone, and he probably outgrosses everybody on Broadway!"[42]

What Andrew Lloyd Webber doesn't realize is that it's not about an organ, a microphone, a stage, or a choir. It's about a God who answers the prayers of His people! I can't tell you how many times I've heard people say: "I walked into the church and I couldn't stop crying." It is because God's presence is here, arresting people's hearts. And it is all the result of prayer.

I therefore encourage you to take time to ponder the question: *Can my prayer life open up prison doors?* Do you truly believe that your prayer life can release someone who has been held in chains and bondage? Will you stir yourself to pray, just like the two women in the Hebrides, or the early church on the eve of Peter's planned execution? The freedom and salvation of countless people may very well depend on the fervency of your prayers!

A CLEAR VOICE NEEDS A CLEAN HEART

A Christian can sin the same sin a sinner sins, but a Christian can't sin the same way a sinner sins. God simply will not allow it. The reason is because the Lord knows not only how costly sin is but how deeply connected it is to our voice, our witness, and His eternal plan—reaching the lost to populate heaven. I've heard it said that "sin will take you farther than you want to go, keep you longer than you want to stay, and cost you more than you want to pay." God knows there is too much at stake to allow sin in our lives—for our sake as well as those we are trying to reach for Christ. That is why the Holy Spirit brings His conviction, addressing sin even while it is in its infant stages.

Lately I have found myself apologizing to my wife a lot. You might even consider it silly if I told you what I have been apologizing for, but God has been convicting me. He wants my heart and mind pure; nothing is too small for Him to go after. It has been as simple as watching a baseball game and a provocative commercial coming on. I felt the Holy Spirit prompting me to turn the channel. Yet when I didn't respond immediately, figuring I would just wait for the next inning to start, at that moment the Holy Spirit said, "Go tell your wife." At one point, I remember objecting before Him, "Enough! There are a lot of people who are worse than me! Why are You picking on me?" But I finally realized this: God is not picking on me.

Instead, He is protecting, purifying, and preparing me. He brought to mind this scripture:

> Let the words of my mouth and the meditation of my heart be acceptable in Thy sight, O Lord. (Psalm 19:14 NASB)

Once we have vision for the lost and start believing for a billion souls, we are the ones God will convict first. He will go after our heart to cleanse it in order to give us a clear voice. I felt the Lord explain to me during those times I felt He was picking on me: "You are the ceiling for what I want to do in this church. I must start with you. I want to deal with those times when you have a wandering mind and a distracted prayer life. I need you to lock in." The Holy Spirit won't allow us to fool around with those wandering thoughts. He will go after them with persistence, even when it is incubating. C. S. Lewis articulates it in a powerful way:

> When I was a child, I have often had a toothache, and I knew that if I went to my mother, she would give me something which would deaden the pain for that night and let me get to sleep. But I did not go to my mother, at least not till the pain became very bad. And the reason I did not go was this: I did not doubt she would give me the aspirin, but I knew she would do something else. I knew she would take me to the dentist the next morning. I could not get what I wanted out of her without getting something more which I did not want. I wanted immediate relief from my pain, but I could not get it without having my teeth set permanently right. And I knew those dentists, I knew they started fiddling about with all sorts of other teeth which had not yet begun to hurt. They would not let sleeping dogs lie. If you gave them an inch, they took a yard.
>
> Our Lord is like the dentist. If you give Him an inch, He

> will take a yard. Dozens of people go to Him to be cured of some one particular sin which they are ashamed of or that which is obviously spotting daily life (like a bad temper or drunkenness). Well, He will cure it alright, but He will not stop there. That may be all you asked, but if you call Him in, He will give you the full treatment.[43]

I have been going to that spiritual dentist lately, and He has been touching things that didn't even hurt yet. But they will. He knows they need to be looked at.

Psalm 51 is like that dentist office. It is a prayer of repentance after David allowed his lustful thoughts to go unchecked, eventually leading him not only to commit adultery but murder as well. This psalm is the prayer of a broken man who blew it. He blew past the convictions, those moments when God was poking around, and went after a situation that literally shattered a good part of his life.

Bear in mind that David was not a new convert. He was a seasoned believer in a powerful position. In 1024 BC when David was a shepherd boy, Samuel the prophet anointed him and announced that he would be the next leader of Israel. Twenty years later, in 1003 BC, David became king of what was considered at the time to be the most powerful nation on the planet. This sin of adultery happened in 993 BC, 30 years since the anointing and calling of God.

It is incredible that over ten years into his reign as king, after experiencing the miracles and favor of God, David lets a wandering eye begin to go beyond wandering and turn into lust, then adultery, and then murder. Suddenly you have a man who has walked with God for more than 30 years beginning to write a psalm of repentance.

God is reminding us that none of us are exempt from being targeted by the enemy. In fact, those who have been walking with God for decades are often prime targets because the enemy wants to silence their voice. He needs the older generation to share their wisdom and tell their story: "I have been young, and now I am old; yet I have not seen the righteous forsaken, or his descendants begging bread" (Psalm 37:25 NASB). The sin may not be adultery; it could be a hidden offense, unforgiveness, feelings of betrayal, even resentment toward the church. These are the subtle snares that can silence our voice.

David Wilkerson was known to say, "Nothing is more tragic than watching a seasoned saint who lost their voice because of bitterness and anger." Sometimes there are people sitting in church with a look on their face that makes it obvious everything has been robbed from them. I have heard it said that sin doesn't age well, but I believe that righteousness does. That's why you will never see a happy old sinner. They grow worse and worse. But you will see good-looking old men and women of God because righteousness begins to mature you, preparing you for heaven. So when God is convicting you of sin, saying, "No, you shouldn't be watching that. Don't look that person up. Don't hold onto that grudge," in your heart, let it go. God is protecting you, purifying you, and preparing you. He is giving you a clean heart so that you can have a clear voice.

Before we get to Psalm 51, let me give you a little backstory. It was less than a year since David committed adultery with a woman named Bathsheba that David wrote this psalm. At the time, Bathsheba was married to an army general named Uriah. David saw her one night and had a one-night stand, and she ended up pregnant. No one knew, so he conjured up a scheme to avoid getting caught. His plan was to bring Uriah home from the battlefield, give him a weekend pass so he could sleep with his wife, and then everyone would assume the baby was his. Of course, the plan failed. David then moved on to plan B which was to put Uriah in the heat of the battle. David instructed his commanding officer to then retreat and let Uriah be killed. David would look like a hero, marrying the mourning widow.

He will fly under the radar, as long as no one does the math of how long they have been married when they begin to see her pregnant.

By the time the child came, nobody seemed to question the timing. Man may have missed it, but God didn't. One day, David is confronted by a prophet named Nathan, and he simply crumbles under the conviction of God. Psalm 51 is David's prayer of repentance. It is a broken man crying out for a second chance. This paraphrase captures his emotions well:

> Generous in love—God, give grace! Huge in mercy—wipe out my bad record. Scrub away my guilt, soak out my sins in your laundry. I know how bad I've been; my sins are staring me down. You're the One I've violated, and you've seen it all, seen the full extent of my evil. You have all the facts before you; whatever you decide about me is fair. I've been out of step with you for a long time, in the wrong since before I was born. What you're after is truth from the inside out. Enter me, then; conceive a new, true life. Soak me in your laundry and I'll come out clean, scrub me and I'll have a snow-white life. Tune me in to foot-tapping songs, set these once-broken bones to dancing. Don't look too close for blemishes, give me a clean bill of health. God, make a fresh start in me, shape a Genesis week from the chaos of my life. Don't throw me out with the trash, or fail to breathe holiness in me. Bring me back from gray exile, put a fresh wind in my sails! (Psalm 51 MSG)

It is important to understand that a clean heart is what makes you effective in winning people to Christ. You being right with God can help get someone else right with God. What is critical and even sobering is the fact that something happens when the heart is not clean: Sin silences the voice of the believer.

There is a phrase in Jeremiah that my heart goes to when I am faced with temptation:

> An appalling and horrible thing Has happened in the land: The prophets prophesy falsely, And the priests rule on their own authority; And My people love it so! But what will you do at the end of it? (Jeremiah 5:30–31 NASB)

Sin only sees what is right before its eyes. Jeremiah awakens the soul and asks, “What will you do at the end of it?” In other words, look at the conclusion. Consider the final cost, not just the present thrill. I often counsel people who are reaping the consequences of sin because they did not pause to consider Jeremiah’s question: “But what will you do when it’s time to pick up the pieces?” (Jeremiah 5:30 MSG).

Psalm 51 is the end of it. Here is a familiar portion of David's prayer:

> Create in me a clean heart, O God, and renew a steadfast spirit within me. Do not cast me away from Your presence, and do not take Your Holy Spirit from me. Restore to me the joy of Your salvation, and uphold me by Your generous Spirit. Then I will teach transgressors Your ways, and sinners shall be converted to You. (Psalm 51:10–13 NKJV)

The end of it for David was that sin robbed him of his voice and effectiveness. When you live in sin that you are unwilling to lay down, your voice becomes silenced in three critical areas: your intercession, your praise, and your testimony.

1. YOUR VOICE IN PRAYER

When there is sin in a believer’s life, the first thing to be affected is their life of intercession. Intercession is a distinct type of prayer—it is praying for others. When a believer is living in sin, their prayers become self-centered. You rarely hear of a person with unconfessed sin who is interceding for the nations and the lost.

Notice David's prayer and how many times "me" or "my" is used:

> Be gracious to me, O God, according to Thy lovingkindness; according to the greatness of Thy compassion blot out my transgressions. Wash me thoroughly from my iniquity, and cleanse me from my sin. For I know my transgressions, and my sin is ever before me. (Psalm 51:1–3 NASB)

> Create in me a clean heart, O God, and renew a steadfast spirit within me. Do not cast me away from Your presence, and do not take Your Holy Spirit from me. Restore to me the joy of Your salvation, and uphold me by Your generous Spirit. (Psalm 51:10–12 NKJV)

Who was David praying for? Himself! David says "me" or "my" nine times in verses 1–3 and six times in verses 10–12. He wasn't thinking of anybody else. Don't let them find me out. God, give me mercy. Help get me through this day. Sin steals intercession from the believer's life. People who are living in sin are simply not concerned about others.

2. YOUR VOICE OF PRAISE

David was a great worshipper. We still sing some of the psalms he wrote to this day. But sin silenced his praise and will cause us to lose our voice of praise as well.

> Deliver me from blood guiltiness, O God, the God of my salvation; then my tongue will joyfully sing of Your righteousness. (Psalm 51:14 NASB)

"Deliver me from my blood guiltiness"—the murder. Notice the "then" of verse 14. David could not sing and praise until the sin was dealt with. He felt dirty and unworthy. You can sing the lyrics and even know them by heart, but they will be empty. Sin turns worship into merely singing songs and playing notes.

3. YOUR VOICE TO WITNESS

The third thing that sin will silence is your voice to witness:

> Create in me a clean heart, O God, and renew a steadfast spirit within me. Do not cast me away from Your presence and do not take Your Holy Spirit from me. Restore to me the joy of Your salvation and sustain me with a willing spirit. Then I will teach transgressors Your ways, and sinners will be converted to You. (Psalm 51:10–13 NASB)

The key is in verse 13 when it says, "Then I will teach transgressors Your ways, and sinners will be converted to You." It implies that David had been teaching transgressors God's ways, but sin caused him to lose his influence among the heathen. He lost his witness and his testimony.

I have watched friends who are great thinkers with letters from universities for their expertise on theological topics, but their hearts were not pure. I watched them have no effect on people's lives. On the other hand, I have seen widows and the elderly without a college degree; all they have is the Holy Ghost, and they will win everybody to Jesus. What's the difference? It's a clean heart, not an educated mind. When the heart is right with God, the voice is clear.

A few years ago, I was in a Christian bookstore with a friend, and a man approached me. I don't know if he knew me, but he abruptly interrupted me and asked, "How many Bible verses have you memorized?" He then proceeded to tell me how many New Testament books he had memorized to classical music. It was both odd and intrusive. Then he kept asking, "How many have you memorized?"

"I've memorized some verses," I responded. But he kept prodding as if he wanted to pit his record against mine to show a clear victory. He wouldn't leave me alone until I gave him a number.

I don't know if it was the Holy Spirit or out of frustration, but I finally said, "I want to ask you a question. With all the verses that you've memorized, how many people have you led to Christ?" Suddenly he got quiet. "You've put all these verses inside of you, but have you shared the gospel? Instead of realizing you won the memorization contest, as if there were one, who is going to heaven because you excelled in this memorization discipline? Don't get me wrong, I think we should memorize the Word and hide it in our hearts. But the purpose is not so we can boast about it."

That man couldn't answer the question. For David, it was adultery and murder that silenced him. For this man, I believe it was his own pride that silenced him. Pride is a devastating sin. Sin robs you of intercession, praise, and powerful witnessing—regardless of what the sin is. That means those who are on a mission to believe for a billion souls must also be on a mission to remain pure before God.

The Bible tells us that 80 years later, they spoke about David's testimony to another king. Don't miss how it is worded:

> But for David's sake the Lord his God gave him a lamp in Jerusalem, to raise up his son after him and to establish Jerusalem; because David did what was right in the sight of the Lord, and had not turned aside from anything that He commanded him all the days of his life, except in the case of Uriah the Hittite. (1 Kings 15:4–5 NASB)

Notice that it does not say, "except in the case of Bathsheba." I would think the Scriptures would mention adultery, but it doesn't. Instead, it says "except in the case of Uriah the Hittite." Adultery was the sin, but the murder was the coverup. It is as if God is saying, "I can forgive sin, but it is coverup that gets judged." Don't try to cover sin up. Unless you lay it down in honesty before the Lord, the burden of it will remain.

It reminds me of what happened in 1987 when New York City reached its landfill capacity. They decided to load a barge carrying 3,000 tons of trash and travel along the Hudson River and the East River, looking for a place to dump it all. They called it the Mobro Barge. They tried to dump the trash in North Carolina, Alabama, and Louisiana, where it was rejected, before going international to Mexico, Belize, and the Bahamas. For five months they sailed with 3,000 tons of trash, searching for a place that would take it—only to end up right back in New York City![44]

That is like the human soul, looking for a place to dump its garbage, yet finding nobody willing to take it. David carried his trash for nine months. He carried a barge of guilt, conviction, and constantly looking over his shoulder. Some people today carry it for years, wandering aimlessly like that barge. King David, with 10 years under his belt, finally comes to the place of asking God to wash him thoroughly. He was a king who wore royal robes, bathed in marble tubs, and slept on silk sheets, yet he felt dirty because sin had soiled his soul and stung his conscience. It saddened his spirit and silenced his praise.

Psalm 51 shows us that the only One willing and able to take our soul's garbage is God Himself.

The Lord says, "Bring it here. I will not only forgive you but change your heart from the inside out." Some people think about all they have done wrong and wonder if God will still forgive them. Satan will try to make you think you're not forgiven so that you will continue to wander for months or years with the burden in your soul, all the while silencing your intercession, praise, and witness. But let me show you a historical record of forgiveness that offers great encouragement.

In the book of Nehemiah, God's people were back from captivity, and now the priests were declaring the forgiveness of God—from creation all the way to the end. Notice what the people do and what God does over and over again. Through it all, God demonstrates His great forgiveness and compassion.

> You saw the affliction of our fathers in Egypt, and heard their cry by the Red Sea. Then You performed signs and wonders against Pharaoh, against all his servants and all the people of his land; for You knew that they acted arrogantly toward them, and made a name for Yourself as it is this day. You divided the sea before them, so they passed through the midst of the sea on dry ground; and their pursuers You hurled into the depths,
>
> like a stone into raging waters. And with a pillar of cloud You led them by day, and with a pillar of fire by night to light for them the way in which they were to go.
>
> Then You came down on Mount Sinai, and spoke with them from heaven; You gave them just ordinances and true laws, good statutes and commandments. So You made known to them Your holy sabbath, and laid down for them commandments, statutes and law, through Your servant Moses. You provided bread from heaven for them for their hunger, You brought forth water from a rock for them for their thirst, and You told them to enter in order to possess the land which You swore to give them.
>
> But they, our fathers, acted arrogantly; they became stubborn and would not listen to Your commandments. They refused to listen, and did not remember Your wondrous deeds which You had performed among them;

so they became stubborn and appointed a leader to return to their slavery in Egypt. But You are a God of forgiveness, gracious and compassionate, slow to anger and abounding in lovingkindness; and You did not forsake them.

Even when they made for themselves a calf of molten metal and said, 'This is your God who brought you up from Egypt,' and committed great blasphemies, You, in Your great compassion, did not forsake them in the wilderness; the pillar of cloud did not leave them by day, to guide them on their way, nor the pillar of fire by night, to light for them the way in which they were to go. You gave Your good Spirit to instruct them, Your manna You did not withhold from their mouth, and You gave them water for their thirst. Indeed, forty years You provided for them in the wilderness and they were not in want; their clothes did not wear out, nor did their feet swell.

You also gave them kingdoms and peoples, and allotted them to them as a boundary. They took possession of the land of Sihon the king of Heshbon and the land of Og the king of Bashan. You made their sons numerous as the stars of heaven, and You brought them into the land which You had told their fathers to enter and possess. So their sons entered and possessed the land. And You subdued before them the inhabitants of the land, the Canaanites, and You gave them into their hand, with their kings and the peoples of the land, to do with them as they desired. They captured fortified cities and a fertile land. They took possession of houses full of every good thing, hewn cisterns, vineyards, olive groves, fruit trees in abundance. So they ate, were filled and grew fat, and reveled in Your great goodness.

But they became disobedient and rebelled against You, and

> cast Your law behind their backs and killed Your prophets who had admonished them so that they might return to You, and they committed great blasphemies. Therefore You delivered them into the hand of their oppressors who oppressed them, but when they cried to You in the time of their distress, You heard from heaven, and according to Your great compassion You gave them deliverers who delivered them from the hand of their oppressors.
>
> But as soon as they had rest, they did evil again before You; therefore You abandoned them to the hand of their enemies, so that they ruled over them. When they cried again to You, You heard from heaven, and many times You rescued them according to Your compassion, and admonished them in order to turn them back to Your law. Yet they acted arrogantly and did not listen to Your commandments but sinned against Your ordinances, by which if a man observes them he shall live. And they turned a stubborn shoulder and stiffened their neck, and would not listen. However, You bore with them for many years, and admonished them by Your Spirit through Your prophets, yet they would not give ear. Therefore You gave them into the hand of the peoples of the lands. Nevertheless, in Your great compassion You did not make an end of them or forsake them, for You are a gracious and compassionate God. (Nehemiah 9:9–31 NASB)

Whenever I read this, I am reminded of how amazing God is. By the time Israel made the golden calf, if I were God, I would have told the people, "Enough is enough. I'm not with you." Yet God says again and again, "I am still with you." Six times in this psalm, we see the word "compassion." In the Hebrew, it means "to carry as a woman carries a baby in her womb." God says, "No matter where you go, I'm carrying you with Me. I won't leave you; I won't forsake you."

If there is any area of your life that is not right with God, it is time to lay it down before Him. He is a compassionate God, ready to forgive and restore. He is willing to create in you a clean heart and renew a right spirit within you, just as He did for David. May you be among the people God is raising up to be His intercessors, worshippers, and witnesses in this hour—those with clean hearts and a clear voice.

FIGHT, FIGHT, MIRACLE

I would like to take you to an Old Testament battle scene that may perplex you at first, but in the end, it will encourage you to persevere in the fight for souls—especially with those people you have already written off as a lost cause. God can lead you to speak to someone, and the conversation may not necessarily go well. When God guides you, it doesn't automatically mean you've met a Nicodemus who is curious and eager to hear the gospel. You have entered into a fight for that person's soul. It's a fight but with a divine plan and strategy. Here are the words I want you to remember: Fight, fight, miracle. Oftentimes, there will be losses before the miracle comes, but don't give up. God is about to do something miraculous.

It has to be the most unusual battle scene I've ever read in the Bible. Yet as I reflected on the verse, I suddenly saw something profoundly helpful for the journey I've been on with people I have been witnessing to. The story is found in Judges 20. This chapter has all the makings of a civil war in Israel with hugely skewed odds: 11 tribes versus one. Israel had a bone to pick with the tribe of Benjamin, the smallest of the 12. Talk about being outnumbered. It was going to be 11 to one, but not just any one—the smallest one!

Here's the backstory: A group of deplorable men who were part of the tribe of Benjamin had raped a Levite's wife and left her dead on her husband's doorstep. The Scriptures tell us that this group of men ravished her all night long (see Judges 19). It was despicable. When the other tribes called for the men to face consequences, these indecent men were protected by Benjamin; they refused to surrender them. At that moment, the battle was on, and that's where the story begins. Eleven tribes were declaring, "We will not tolerate this injustice. If you won't deal with it, we will!"

> Then all the sons of Israel from Dan to Beersheba, including the land of Gilead, came out, and the congregation assembled as one man to the Lord at Mizpah. The chiefs of all the people, even of all the tribes of Israel, took their stand in the assembly of the people of God, 400,000 foot soldiers who drew the sword. (Judges 20:1–2 NASB)

> The sons of Benjamin gathered from the cities to Gibeah, to go out to battle against the sons of Israel. From the cities on that day the sons of Benjamin were numbered, 26,000 men who draw the sword. (Judges 20:14–15 NASB)

Keep in mind the battlefield numbers because they will be important later: Benjamin had 26,000 soldiers, and Israel had 400,000. Here is the part of the battle that is puzzling: Israel is in the right to fight this battle. They went to God and asked Him for wisdom, meaning prayer was involved. In fact, they asked God three times, and three times He directs them. God's voice is speaking, and it seems that He is moving.

> Now the sons of Israel arose, went up to Bethel, and inquired of God and said, "Who shall go up first for us to battle against the sons of Benjamin?" Then the Lord said, "Judah shall go up first." So the sons of Israel arose in the morning and camped against Gibeah. The men of Israel went out to battle against Benjamin, and the men of Israel

> arrayed for battle against them at Gibeah. Then the sons of Benjamin came out of Gibeah and felled to the ground on that day 22,000 men of Israel. But the people, the men of Israel, encouraged themselves and arrayed for battle again in the place where they had arrayed themselves the first day. The sons of Israel went up and wept before the Lord until evening, and inquired of the Lord, saying, "Shall we again draw near for battle against the sons of my brother Benjamin?" And the Lord said, "Go up against him." Then the sons of Israel came against the sons of Benjamin the second day. Benjamin went out against them from Gibeah the second day and felled to the ground again 18,000 men of the sons of Israel; all these drew the sword. Then all the sons of Israel and all the people went up and came to Bethel and wept; thus they remained there before the Lord and fasted that day until evening. And they offered burnt offerings and peace offerings before the Lord. The sons of Israel inquired of the Lord (for the ark of the covenant of God was there in those days, and Phinehas the son of Eleazar, Aaron's son, stood before it to minister in those days), saying, "Shall I yet again go out to battle against the sons of my brother Benjamin, or shall I cease?" And the Lord said, "Go up, for tomorrow I will deliver them into your hand." (Judges 20:18–28 NASB)

They keep praying, God keeps speaking, yet they keep losing. I have read this story over the years and wondered, "What in the world is going on?" God clearly instructed them to go. He even told them to send Judah first; it seemed like He had a strategy. Nevertheless, they were defeated and lost 22,000 men in the first battle. When they asked the second time, God told them to go up again, and they end up losing 18,000 more men. That's 40,000 men lost in the first two battles. At that point, I would be thinking, "Are we even hearing from God? Or is there an Achan in the camp—some sin among us?" By the third time, they went from inquiring and weeping to fasting and offering burnt offerings and peace offerings. Finally they ask God for the third time, "Shall I yet again go out to battle against the sons of my brother Benjamin, or shall I cease?" (verse 28). I don't blame them for adding those last four words: "or shall I cease?" I would've really emphasized that part—"or are we missing something here?" The Lord answers, "Go up. I'm going to deliver them into your hand."

I'm not so sure I would go up boldly, but they did, and they won a decisive victory.

> And the Lord struck Benjamin before Israel, so that the sons of Israel destroyed 25,100 men of Benjamin that day, all who draw the sword. (Judges 20:35 NASB)

They killed 25,100 of the 26,000. Israel decimated them, taking out 97% of Benjamin in the third battle!

This story left me wrestling with a few questions: Why did it take two losses to get a victory? Why did God give them two green lights to fight that ended up being two devastating losses? Then I started asking: Does every green light to move forward guarantee a victory? Or can I move forward, lose, and it still be God moving me forward?

And then the final question: What does this have to do with winning a billion souls?

Let's look once again at the third confrontation. There is something about this battle that I want you to notice:

> The sons of Benjamin went out against the people and were drawn away from the city, and they began to strike and kill some of the people. (Judges 20:31 NASB)

In the previous battles, they fought from inside the walls, but during the third battle, Benjamin was lured out of his fortified walls and city. The Benjamites seem to get overconfident after killing 40,000, so now they are leaving their walled city to go into battle. That is when Israel gives them some ground.

> The sons of Benjamin said, "They are struck down before us, as at the first." But the sons of Israel said, "Let us flee that we may draw them away from the city to the highways." Then all the men of Israel... in ambush broke out of their place, even out of Maareh-geba. When ten thousand choice men from all Israel came against Gibeah, the battle became fierce; but Benjamin did not know that disaster was close to them. And the Lord struck Benjamin before Israel, so that the sons of Israel destroyed 25,100 men of Benjamin that day, all who draw the sword. So the sons of Benjamin saw that they were defeated. When the men of Israel gave ground to Benjamin because they relied on the men in ambush whom they had set against Gibeah, the men in ambush hurried and rushed against Gibeah; the men in ambush also deployed and struck all the city with the edge of the sword. Now the appointed sign between the men of Israel and the men in ambush was that they would make a great cloud of smoke rise from the city. Then the men of Israel turned in the battle, and Benjamin began to strike and kill about thirty men of Israel, for they said, "Surely they are defeated before us, as in the first battle." But when the cloud began to rise from the city in a column of smoke, Benjamin looked behind them; and behold, the whole city was going up in smoke to heaven. Then the men of Israel turned, and the men of Benjamin were terrified; for they saw that disaster was close to them. (Judges 20:32–41 NASB)

God's strategy for battle three was to lure the Benjamites away from their walls, give them some ground, and then ambush them and take down those walls.

So how does this relate to winning a billion souls? It reminds us that not every Jesus conversation will be as fast and simple as the one between Jesus and the woman at the well, Philip and the Ethiopian, or Jesus and Nicodemus. In fact, many conversations along the way will leave you feeling discouraged. That's why we must keep in mind that it usually takes time to win someone to Christ.

Why does it often take time and loss before the miracle happens? It is because worldviews are walls. They are what people hide behind when confronted with truth. Many people today are entrenched in unbiblical worldviews and lifestyles full of bondage and chains. It may take some fights to get them away from those walls. Even Solomon, the richest and wisest man who ever lived, concluded: "A rich man's wealth is his strong city, and like a high wall in his own imagination" (Proverbs 18:11 NASB). It may take what feel like losses in conversations in order to lure people away from the fortress of their own "truth." But breakthrough is always possible.

Lee Strobel was a successful legal editor of *The Chicago Tribune* who became a Christian in 1981. He was previously an atheist but was prompted to investigate the claims of Jesus when his wife got saved. Instead of just blasting her, he decided to go on a two-year journey of investigating the evidences and claims of Jesus Christ to see if what she believed was true. As a result, he came to Christ and wrote a powerful book called *The Case for Christ*.

He later conducted interviews with people who had been on a journey like his. In his book called *The Case for Faith,* Strobel does an interview with a preacher who turned agnostic. And not just any preacher—Charles Templeton, the traveling companion of Billy Graham. In 1946, they both started preaching around the country together. However, they went separate ways two years later because of Templeton's view that the Bible wasn't inerrant nor infallible. Billy Graham went on to become the greatest evangelist of our generation, literally leading millions of people to Christ. Meanwhile, Templeton was left teetering between agnosticism and atheism. Agnostics believe it is unknown whether or not God exists; atheists have definitively concluded there is no God. Templeton eventually wrote a book called *Farewell to God: My Reasons for Rejecting the Christian Faith.*

Strobel ended up interviewing him one year before Templeton died. During the interview, Templeton was behind the agnostic walls he had hidden behind for over 50 years. He pointed to his evidence of why he doesn't believe in a good God, including the horrors of Alzheimer's disease which he was battling. He described in gripping detail the way it hideously strips people of their personal identity by rotting their mind and memory. "How," he demanded, "could a compassionate God allow such a ghastly illness to torture its victims and their loved ones?" The answer, he concluded, was simple: Alzheimer's would not exist if there were a loving God. And because it does exist, that's one more bit of persuasive evidence that God does not.

Strobel began to walk through this with him. Remember, worldviews are walls, and for Templeton, it all started with him doubting God. Long before Alzheimer's set in, it was pictures he saw in magazines of famine and suffering that caused him to doubt. As Strobel asked him questions, Templeton pushed back. The 83-year-old man put up his walls against Strobel, but Strobel continued to ask. Of course, the Holy Spirit is always at work, ready to set an ambush. Near the end of the interview, Strobel finally asked the agnostic-turned-atheist this question: "What do you think about Jesus today?" Here is Strobel's account of the answer he received:

> "He was," Templeton began, "the greatest human being who has ever lived. He was the intrinsically wisest person I've ever encountered. . . . Everything decent I know, I learned from Him. . . . There's no question he had the highest moral standard, the least duplicity, the greatest compassion, of any human being in history.... There have been many other wonderful people, but Jesus is Jesus. He is the most important human being who has ever existed."
>
> That's when Templeton suddenly uttered the words I never expected to hear from him. "And if I may put it this way," he said as his voice began to crack, "I . . . miss . . . Him!" With that, tears flooded his eyes. He turned his head and looked downward, raising his left hand to shield his face from me. His shoulders bobbed as he wept. *What was going on?* Was this an unguarded glimpse into his soul?[45]

He was coming out from behind the wall. Strobel gave him some ground. He knew it was a fight, but suddenly Templeton's soul was laid open on the battlefield. He thought he was winning with his Alzheimer's case. He thought he was winning with pain and suffering, but when Strobel simply asked him about Jesus, he peered out from beneath the walled city. And when talking about Jesus, something began to hit his heart. Without even knowing it, Templeton was ambushed.

I've gotten it all wrong over the years in evangelism. I thought the fight meant to move on because the person is not interested. On the contrary, this is what I've learned: The fight is proof that their walls are not impregnable, and hell is starting to wake up as you start speaking truth to them.

Have you ever had conversations with friends and family, and each one seemed like a defeat? They weren't interested in Jesus. They didn't think they needed forgiveness of sin. They dug in their heels and declared God doesn't exist. Each time you left the conversation, you felt another loss and began to wonder if it's time for you to back down. But the fight is not because nothing is happening; it's because God is working. Remember, when you are speaking truth to someone who is on the verge of being released from hell's chains, you are fighting hell to get them on the other side of those walls. Those conversations are battlegrounds. People have walls; people will be combative. It's a spiritual fight to bring somebody to faith. That's what happened with Israel. God told them to go, and they lost a lot in the first two battles. But then came the miracle.

In most cases, it will be a journey with people. You will lose some arguments, but don't get discouraged; you are drawing them out in the open for a Holy Ghost ambush. The Bible says in Proverbs 11:30, "He who wins souls is wise" (NKJV). The word "wise" is used to describe someone who is skilled or experienced. In other words, a wise soul winner is a seasoned fighter who is skilled in spiritual warfare. When you start speaking truth, truth cracks the walls and breaks through those situations.

I came across a powerful example of this in an email we received from a member of one of our "Beyond Sunday" Connect Groups. As she began sharing truth with a woman at a bus stop, the walls began to come down:

> I obeyed the nudge at a bus stop. I wouldn't have been as keen to follow through except for Pastor Tim's message that the Beyond Sunday group went through that day.
>
> After I got home, I went back outside to return an item to the store. While waiting for the bus to return home, I checked the bus schedule and had nine minutes to wait for the next bus. I noticed Robin sitting in the bus stand

smoking a cigarette. My first thought was, “Can't sit there, don't want to inhale smoke,” so I remained standing at a distance. I looked over again and noticed how lonely she looked to me sitting there puffing, looking off into the distance. Then came the nudge from the Holy Spirit.

The next time I looked I thought, “I have nine minutes left, there's no one directly around her, I should go over and speak with her.” Another minute or so passed by; finally, I walked over to her and said, “Hello, I noticed you sitting here, can I pray for you?” She said yes. I asked what her name was and told her mine. Then I asked her if there was anything in particular she wanted me to pray for, and her request was that God would bless her with whatever He thought she needed.

After I prayed, she thanked me. Then I remembered from our group to ask as an introduction question to sharing the gospel, so I asked Robin what would she say to God if she died tomorrow and faced Him and He asked her why He should let her into His heaven. Robin told me she hoped God would let her in because of her good deeds.

Then I morphed into full Pastor Tim mode and told her that good deeds were good; but that's not what Jesus said would make her acceptable. He said that she must be born again because no man can enter the Kingdom of God unless they are born again. Then I explained the A, B, Cs to her and asked if she would pray with me to receive Christ as her Savior and Lord.

She was somewhat resistant because the self-righteousness was still on display, so I said to her:

How do you know that your good deeds are good

> enough for God?
>
> Anything we could give to God is His that He's given to us.
>
> The Bible says our righteousness is as filthy rags to God.
>
> If we reject the Son, we reject the Father, too.
>
> Surprisingly, this seemed to make sense to her so when I asked her again, she agreed to pray with me and asked Jesus to forgive her sins and come into her heart.
>
> The bus was approaching so I gave her one of TSC's "You're invited" calling cards I always carry with me. When she saw Times Square Church her face lit up in recognition. Unlike Philip, the Spirit of the Lord did not carry me away, the MTA bus did, but I also went on my way rejoicing.

Sometimes the "fight, fight, miracle" can happen in nine minutes like at that bus stop, but sometimes it can take decades. Amy, my assistant, shared with our staff about the incredible conversion of her mom. Amy has been born again for 23 years, and it has been 23 years of her asking her mom, "If you die today, do you know where you're going?" Her mom would always say no because in her mind, salvation was based on works. She would have to make sure God liked her enough and that her works were pleasing to Him.

But this Holy Week, Amy walked her mom through John 3:16 word by word, and then she read in the Bible about the conversation Jesus had with the thief on the cross. Jesus said in the end, "Today, you'll be with Me in paradise" (see Luke 23:43). That thief on the cross couldn't do a single good thing except receive the promise of Jesus. Her mom then came to the conclusion that the thief gained heaven because he believed Jesus was the Savior wrongfully being hung.

At that point, Amy asked again, "Mom, if you die today, do you know where you are going?"

Her mother replied, "Yes." When Amy asked why, she said, "Because like the thief, I believe it's by faith alone, not works!"

Amy's mom had hidden behind the walls of her religion for 23 years. Yet after 23 years of speaking to her about the Lord, she was finally drawn out because truth cracks those walls!

I was speaking with Nicky Cruz recently and asked him, "How long was it from the moment David Wilkerson came to New York City until you got saved?" I didn't know the answer because when you read *The Cross and the Switchblade* or watch the movie, it seems like it might have been months or even years.

Nicky answered, "Davie was here for two weeks, and then I got saved. The first time I came in contact with him was on the streets of Brooklyn at an outdoor street rally. That's when Davie met my dad. Davie came down off that stage, came to me and put out his hand and said, 'Nicky, I'd like to shake your hand and tell you that God loves you.' And I slapped him in the face and spat on him."

That's losing the first battle massively, like Israel losing 22,000 men.

"What about the second encounter?" I asked.

He said, "I don't know who it was. Someone told Davie where I lived. He showed up in the middle of the night to tell me that Jesus loves me. I cursed him out and slammed the door."

That's loss number two. If I had gotten slapped and spat upon, I would've concluded, "I don't think they want to hear the gospel."

It seemed to be getting nowhere, and David kept getting abused, but something inside of him refused to give up. It was like the Israelites asking God about that third battle, "God, do I go out again, or do You want me to cease?" God began to speak to David to go to the upper west side of Manhattan, rent out St. Nicholas Arena, invite all the gangs of New York City to come, and advertise that there would be no cops there. All the gangs and no cops? It sounded like he was out of his mind! But somehow David thought it was a good idea. He knew that the Holy Ghost was about to set an ambush to bring these gangs to Christ.

David sent out the invitation, and all the gangs must have thought it would be the perfect opportunity to have an all-out gang fight. However, going to St. Nicholas Arena meant the gangs were about to leave their fortified walls. They didn't realize that in their headquarters in the basements of Brooklyn and the Bronx, they were hidden behind their walls, their colors and their jackets. Yet David was believing for a miracle. He stood there until they were lured out into the open. Nicky was standing in the middle of the battlefield like Benjamin, unaware that God spoke to David to preach about the cross of Jesus Christ that night.

I asked Nicky, "What was it? God wanted to get you born again so that you could lead millions of people to Christ in our generation. God knew what you were supposed to be, but hell was fighting against it."

Nicky said, "Davie kept speaking about the cross—how Jesus did nothing but good to people, that He just loved people, yet they killed and crucified Him. Something in me thought, 'That's not fair. It's not right what they did to this man.' And as I kept hearing the cross, it kept melting my heart." Why? Because Nicky was out from behind the walls. Truth was coming like a sledgehammer to knock down those walls. All of a sudden as David was preaching that night, Nicky Cruz got saved. It had been two weeks of battles and losses. It was a slap, a spit, and then finally a salvation took place that night!

Nicky's story as well as the story in Judges began to challenge me as

I thought about some neighbors I've been witnessing to. I recently took a neighbor from our apartment building out and talked to him about Christ. He is from another country, works at the UN, and is an agnostic. As I was speaking to him, I realized I was speaking to a man who lived behind a wall. He wouldn't hear anything I had to say. My initial reaction was, "OK, I'm done. He's not budging. There are other people who are hungry for truth that I should be talking to." But I felt the Lord say, "No, I want you to fight. Fight, fight, and then the miracle. Take him out again." I'm ready for a fight on this one, but I'm going to continue to speak truth to crack those walls.

There is another guy I've been ministering to at the gym. I've never heard anybody drop so many F-bombs in my life. He can't seem to use a phrase without profanity. Every time we talk, I'm thinking, "OK, I've had enough of this." But in this case as well, God is reminding me, "That's the fight. You have to lure him out and let Me do My work inside of him."

First conversations may feel like you are losing ground, but keep praying and believing for the breakthrough. You are going to hear fighting words from behind the walls, "I prayed before and nothing happened. There is no God." They may scream at you, "If God loved me, why did He take my mom?" or "Religion is a private thing." Satan will not release them from the chains of hell without a fight, and you are commissioned to fight for their souls.

Looking around at our society, I have come to this conclusion: The acceleration of evil gets men to dead ends faster, so they need God sooner. Many are arguing about how we are legalizing too many things that are contrary to God's ways, but it doesn't bring fear to me. Do you know what the legalization of sin does? It gets people to dead ends sooner, and they are going to need God faster. That's what is happening in our culture—all of it is bringing us closer to God. But it is going to require a fight. When you're witnessing and the conversation gets heated or controversial, don't assume it's over. It usually means the miracle is not far away. So don't give up; don't be discouraged. Fight, fight, and then the miracle!

FIRE SNATCHERS

Just a few months after it occurred, it seemed most of the world had already forgotten what took place in Los Angeles in January 2025. Southern California experienced the most devastating winter wildfires in its history. The fires tore through Los Angeles, resulting in 29 deaths, numerous injuries, 16,000 structures burned to the ground, and 50,000 acres destroyed. Thousands were forced to evacuate areas of the Pacific Palisades and Eaton Canyon. Officials said they hadn't seen destruction like this in four decades, with damage estimates climbing toward $200 billion. Thousands of firefighters from throughout the U.S. battled those flames across 45 square miles as it burned for 24 days.[46]

When the fires reached their worst, they would call in an elite group of firefighters called Hotshots. These men and women are trained to go straight into a wall of hell—to fight the fire where it is raging at its hottest. The pictures and rare footage I saw of these men and women putting their lives on the line brought shivers to my soul.

I come from a family of policemen and firemen, but this is an entirely different breed of firemen. There are only around 100 Hotshot crews in the US. A Hotshot crew is typically 18–25 elite firefighters who respond to the hottest, most dangerous part of the fire.[47] While people are running away, they are running into it. I read one of the Hotshot stories that described how they were carving a burned area to stop the flames from reaching down to the town. The fire was moving so quickly that from 200 yards away, they could hear the noise building. Embers were flying through the air, starting new fires all around. Then they began to hear a particular sound: Out of control wildfires bearing down on you make a sound like a hundred freight trains coming at you. When you hear that sound, it is basically over for you.

One of the Hotshots reportedly said, "When we heard that sound, we knew the fire was coming at us, and we'd either be dead or suffer a hundred percent of body burns. At that moment, we had no other options. My partner was shouting, his voice being sucked in by the howling of the fire. Our brothers were on the other side of the wall. I saw daylight and the asphalt where the fire couldn't burn, but I just couldn't get there. Suddenly out of nowhere, I had this arm reach through this wall, grab me, and jerk me to clean air. We sucked it in greedily. I felt pure joy surging through me knowing that we got out alive."

An arm came through the wall of fire and pulled him out! This is the kind of people we want to be in the spirit—those who jerk others from the flames of hell so they can breathe heaven and feel joy again. In fact, the Bible speaks of another group of "Hotshots." Their names are in the book of Jude, and this is their training:

> But you, beloved, building yourselves up on your most holy faith; praying in the Holy Spirit; keep yourselves in the love of God, waiting anxiously for the mercy of our Lord Jesus Christ to eternal life. And have mercy on some, who are doubting. (Jude 20–22 NASB)

These spiritual Hotshots are constantly praying in the Holy Ghost, not waiting for music to move them. They keep themselves in the love of God and are waiting for the second coming. All of this is part of their training so that they will be ready to run into the firestorm. Jude describes their task this way:

> Save others, snatching them out of the fire. (Jude 23 NASB)

We may not be Hotshots, but we are all called to be trained as something even more urgent—what Jude might call "fire snatchers." When it comes to souls, fire snatchers are those who rescue people from the deadly flames.

Which fire is Jude referring to? Solomon answers the question for us, using fire and sin simultaneously:

> For a prostitute will bring you to poverty, but sleeping with another man's wife will cost you your life. Can a man scoop a flame into his lap and not have his clothes catch on fire? Can he walk on hot coals and not blister his feet? So it is with the man who sleeps with another man's wife. Proverbs 6:26–29 (NLT)

Solomon describes that fire wall in terms of immorality and adultery. So Jude gives us the calling: fire snatchers. Solomon gives us the name of the fire: sin. But it is Abraham who gives us the tools for how to do the fire snatching.

The book of Genesis tells us about how Abraham stepped into the heat of the battle in order to rescue his nephew Lot. Lot ended up in trouble because of the choices he had made. When he and Abraham decided to part ways, Lot got to choose first where he wanted to live.

> Lot lifted up his eyes and saw all the valley of the Jordan, that it was well watered everywhere—this was before the Lord destroyed Sodom and Gomorrah—like the garden of the Lord, like the land of Egypt as you go to Zoar. So Lot chose for himself all the valley of the Jordan; and Lot

> journeyed eastward. Thus they separated from each other. Abram settled in the land of Canaan, while Lot settled in the cities of the valley, and moved his tents as far as Sodom. Now the men of Sodom were wicked exceedingly and sinners against the Lord. And the Lord said to Abram, after Lot had separated from him, "Now lift up your eyes and look from the place where you are, northward and southward and eastward and westward; for all the land which you see, I will give it to you and to your descendants forever. I will make your descendants as the dust of the earth, so that if anyone can number the dust of the earth, then your descendants can also be numbered. Arise, walk about the land through its length and breadth; for I will give it to you." (Genesis 13:10–17 NASB)

Lot chooses Sodom and moves his tents that way. Isn't it interesting that as soon as the separation took place, the Lord spoke to Abraham? While Lot lifted his eyes and saw Sodom, Abraham lifted his eyes and saw the four corners of the earth. Sometimes we need to separate from people who only see what is right in front of their eyes so that God can show us bigger things. That is when we begin to see what is possible, to see what God sees.

Lot moves to Sodom, and in less than a year, the city is under attack. Five kings came against them:

> Now the valley of Siddim was full of tar pits; and the kings of Sodom and Gomorrah fled, and they fell into them. But those who survived fled to the hill country. Then [the enemy] took all the goods of Sodom and Gomorrah and all their food supply, and departed. They also took Lot, Abram's nephew, and his possessions and departed, for he was living in Sodom. (Genesis 14:10–12 NASB)

Sodom was a fire hazard. Lot was living in a place that was flammable, doing exactly what Solomon warned about: "Can a man scoop a flame into his lap and not have his clothes catch on fire?" (Proverbs 6:27 NLT). Lot was playing around with relationships and wicked behaviors, refusing to believe that he would get burned. Yet suddenly he found himself stuck behind the fire wall, in need of a fire snatcher to reach through and rescue him.

When Abraham heard that Lot was taken captive, he suited up and got ready to take action.

> When Abram heard that his relative had been taken captive, he led out his trained men, born in his house, three hundred and eighteen, and went in pursuit as far as Dan. He divided his forces against them by night, he and his servants, and defeated them, and pursued them as far as Hobah, which is north of Damascus. He brought back all the goods, and also brought back his relative Lot with his possessions, and also the women, and the people. (Genesis 14:14–16 NASB)

Remember, Jude tells us to "save others, snatching them out of the fire" (Jude 23 NASB). "Snatching" means "to come with a force and to pull out." Interestingly, it is the same word used when the Bible says we will be "caught up" in the rapture.

> Then we who are alive and remain will be caught up together with them in the clouds to meet the Lord in the air, and so we shall always be with the Lord. (1 Thessalonians 4:17 NASB)

Our job is to reach through and snatch people out of the fire so they can ultimately be caught up in the rapture. How exactly do we do this? There are some powerful principles we can learn by looking at how Abraham snatches Lot out when he was taken captive.

Think for a moment of one person you know on the other side of that fire wall—someone who is on their way to hell unless someone rescues them. With that person in mind, let's see what we can learn from Abraham.

1. GET ALL THE HELP YOU NEED.

> He led out his trained men, born in his house, three hundred and eighteen. (Genesis 14:14 NASB)

Abraham did not go alone. There are times when you are dealing with someone who is caught in the fire, and you need all the help you can get in order to rescue them. Find people who will pray and believe with you. Have people share a testimony with that individual. Let people text them, simply saying, "Praying for you." Don't do it by yourself. If you have a prodigal child, get as many people as you can praying for your sons and daughters because they are caught in hell's trap. Remember, you are not alone. You have the body of Christ to help you. When people ask you what they can pray for, tell them who you are praying for. Tell them that you need them to be one of the 318.

I'll never forget what happened some years ago in our Detroit church. One of our leaders had been free from crack cocaine for ten years. He used to tell me how every day when he went to work, he had a choice. If he turned right, he would get to the bus stop to go to his job that he worked at for ten years. If he turned left, two blocks down was the crack house that held him in bondage.

In other words, he was two blocks away from entering into the hottest part of the fire. This was a man with a beautiful wife and godly kids. And he said to me, "I decided one day to turn left." Instead of getting on the bus to go to work, he walked the two blocks back to an addiction—right into the firestorm. His wife called me and said, "My husband is back at the crack house. I can tell you where it's at, but he won't come out, and they won't let him out. Will you go to the crack house and get him?"

I thought to myself, "If I'm going to that crack house, I'm getting my 318 men!" I picked two of the biggest men in our church. Not only were these men full of the Holy Ghost, they also worked out. I walked up to that crack house with these two men and knocked on the door. A small slot in the door slid open, revealing a peephole. I said, "I'm Pastor Tim. We know he's in there. Send him out!" The next thing I knew, they shut the peephole, the door cracked open, and they shoved that man out so fast. I grabbed him, took him home, and he started the journey toward freedom. Don't be afraid to get whatever help you need in order to grab people out of that fire!

2. DON'T JUST GET ANYONE, GET THE TRAINED.

He led out his trained men. (Genesis 14:14 NASB)

Abraham didn't take just anyone, he got the trained. Some sin is so deep-seated that we don't need just anybody; we need those who have been trained for this. For example, I am so thankful for the men and women who lead our Teen Challenge and Victory Outreach centers around the world. They help people break addictions and life-controlling situations by the power of Jesus Christ.

Firefighting is difficult, but here is what I have been praying lately: "Lord, teach me to be a smoke detector, not just the fire department." Those things on your ceiling are called smoke alarms, not fire alarms. If it's a fire alarm, it's already over and you're dead. But smoke is a warning that something is about to happen. We need the ability to smell smoke—in a marriage, on our children, in our church—so we can see God begin to move before this thing becomes a deadly fire. And when you act immediately, you have time to get the right people involved to help.

3. YOU CAN BE TRAINED, BUT WE MUST KNOW ABOUT YOUR BIRTH.

In order to be part of this deliverance, you must carry two birth certificates. That's because as a fire snatcher, you need to know not only the day you were born but also the day that you were born again.

> When Abram heard that his relative had been taken captive, he led out his trained men, born in his house, three hundred and eighteen. (Genesis 14:14 NASB)

Notice that Abraham's trained men were "born in his house." To be a fire snatcher, you have to be born in God's house—born again. Let me explain it like this: Be careful about using people who believe in Freud but don't believe in Lucifer. You can approach all these issues from a textbook perspective but never go deep enough to where the forces of hell are working to control people's lives. Being trained in counseling and psychology is valuable, but it doesn't necessarily mean you know how to do fire snatching. Fire is not a symptom; fire is a bondage that wants to drag people to hell. We need people who have been born in God's house to snatch souls out of the flames. We don't need to just talk to them about principles. We need to snatch them from death and set them free by the power of God. James put it this way:

> Therefore, confess your sins to one another, and pray for one another so that you may be healed. The effective prayer of a righteous man can accomplish much. (James 5:16 NASB)

Just because you ask someone to pray doesn't mean their prayers are effective. You need to make sure it is a righteous man or woman who knows how to get ahold of God. I am very careful not to say to just anyone, "Hey, pray for me." I'm going to the people who live righteously and know how to pray with faith and authority.

I recently received this testimony from a member of our

security team:

> A few weeks ago, I was bleeding internally and passed out. I was rushed to the ER and released a few hours later. But it happened again the next day, so I was rushed back to the ER bleeding again. They kept me 4 days and then released me. But soon I was rushed back to the hospital and admitted again. I received 5 blood transfusions in 9 days. While in the hospital, I watched the 10 a.m. Sunday service on my phone. Before Pastor Tim preached, he asked anyone who needs healing to raise their hands, and he prayed for them. I raised my hands in my hospital bed. During this time, I was reminded of the woman with an issue of blood in Luke 8:43 who touched the hem of Jesus's garment. I believed that God would heal me too, so I prayed and asked Jesus to transform a hospital robe into the garment the woman in the Bible touched as a point of contact. I held that robe in my hand, and I have not had any more bleeding since. The Lord healed me that day and I was released from the hospital that evening! The doctor apologized for not having a diagnosis or explanation.

Of course, we have the explanation: Jesus! I believe God uses doctors, but also believe in Dr. Jesus. We need doctors, but we need miracles. We need people not only with degrees, but people who know they need a miracle and where it comes from. God can use counselors and doctors, but when the miracle is needed, there isn't a diagnosis or a textbook that will suffice. We need heaven to show up when somebody is in a fire. Get help, get the trained, get the two-birth-certificate people, and get the lost out of that fire.

4. PURSUE, DON'T WAIT TO BE ASKED FOR HELP.

Notice that Lot never asked for help. Abraham heard about what happened and moved into action. The longer you wait, the more the fire will consume. Remember, fires can move like a locomotive, destroying everything in its path. Make the phone call, send the text, talk to them and say, "I'm praying for you today."

On July 4th, my family had the opportunity to go to Queens for the Subway Series between the Mets and the Yankees. Sadly, it wasn't a great day for us Yankees fans. After the game, we had to go home with thousands of people trying to cram onto the 7 train. We stood in line and soon realized that we were on the wrong platform. We were on the local platform, which meant 15 stops before we would even get to Manhattan. On the other side was the 7 Express, which would get us home in just a few stops. An express train was arriving in a few minutes, meaning we would have to go back down the stairs, make our way through the crowd again, come back up, and hopefully make the train. Everyone in my family agreed it would be worth it, except for me. I didn't want to run. The doors opened on the local 7 train and I said, "Let's stay."

"Dad, we're going." I was totally outvoted. So this 61-year-old man had to run down the stairs, through the people, back up the stairs, and as soon as we got to the platform, the train pulled up and the doors opened. We were about to get into the car right at the top of the steps where everybody else was packing in, but I suggested the next car instead. It was providence. We walked right into a firestorm. A man was yelling and cursing at the people in the seats. While everybody was moving to the back of the train, I'm going, "Hallelujah, we are in the right train!"

It looked combative, but I felt like we were supposed to stay and go into the fire. So I did. I put my hand on the man who was cursing at another couple. He had a Mets jersey on. I said, "Listen, you already won today. Let's be joyful. Let's not do this." All of a sudden, God showed up on the 7 express train, and the guy says to me, "What's your story? What do you do?" The entire time, his wife was whispering to me, “Thank you!”

I replied, “I'm a pastor in Manhattan, in a church across the street from Wicked.”

He looked at his wife and said, “Let's give him money.”

“Hold on, we don't want any money.”

Then he looked at my son-in-law and asked, “Did you become spiritual when you went to that church?”

“No, it's not a spiritual thing,” my son-in-law explained. “We don't even like to use that word. It's a relationship with Jesus that you need.” Clearly my daughter married well.

The couple was blown away. Not only was the situation diffused, God was glorified. It was a fire-snatching moment on the 7 train. No one asked for help; no one asked for us to step in. I understand that the situation could have gone very wrong, but I knew that it was an opportunity and God was showing me, “There's a fire. Don't wait to be invited. You get into that thing.” While everybody else was backing away, God wanted to show up. You just pursue. You never know what God will do when you go and believe Him. Maybe He will allow you to reach your hand through a fire wall and jerk someone out. This man who wanted to beat up a couple ended up hugging us before he got off the train!

5. EVERY FIGHT IS A NIGHT FIGHT.

> He divided his forces against them by night. (Genesis 14:15 NASB)

Every fight for a soul is a night fight. At night, darkness is involved. But always remember this: Hell is strong, but God is stronger. It reminds me of the lyrics to the song “Stronger”:

> *Faithfulness, none can deny*

Through the storm, and through the fire
There is truth that sets me free
Jesus Christ, who lives in me
You are stronger, you are stronger
Sin is broken, You have saved me
It is written, Christ is risen
Jesus, You are Lord of all.[48]

God is always stronger than any work of darkness, so do not fear even when it is a night fight. Genesis 14:15 goes on to say:

> . . . he and his servants, and defeated them, and pursued them as far as Hobah, which is north of Damascus. He brought back all the goods, and also brought back his relative Lot with his possessions, and also the women, and the people. (Genesis 14:15–16 NASB)

When you break through the fire wall, God moves. It was a night fight, but Lot was rescued!

Fire snatching is not for the faint of heart. Remember, you will need help—and not just any help, but the right help. You will need to find those who have been trained and have been born again. Being a fire snatcher will also require courage to pursue as well as endurance to persevere through the night fight.

In those moments when the cost of being a fire snatcher might seem overwhelming, remember the extreme price Jesus paid to snatch us from the fire of sin and the grip of hell. As it says in Isaiah 53:11, "When he sees all that is accomplished by his anguish, he will be satisfied" (NLT). To be a fire snatcher is to follow Jesus into the heat, knowing that what is accomplished through that sacrifice will be worth it all.

GO, STAND, SPEAK (THAT'S WHAT COMES AFTER FREEDOM)

I have come to the conclusion that the Christian life is a lot like a rollercoaster. When you say "yes" to Jesus, get ready for a wild ride for the rest of your life. It goes up; it goes down. You have to buckle up and secure all loose items every single day. You will scream, you will laugh, and at times, you will think you are about to die. But rest assured, Jesus will be with you the entire time.

Acts chapter 5 reads like a rollercoaster full of ups and downs. Acts 4 ends with an offering being taken up, and a man named Barnabas generously giving his gift. The rollercoaster was on its way up. However, Acts 5 opens with Ananias and Sapphira lying about their offering, and the rollercoaster plunges as they die because of their sin. The rollercoaster then goes back up as healings and miracles abound, and the church begins to grow. Shortly after, the apostles are put in jail—another drop back down. In the middle of the night, the apostles are miraculously delivered by an angel—back up. Then they were brought back into custody by the officials—down it goes again. However, the apostles end up preaching to the Sanhedrin, the most powerful group of Jewish people—back up again. After that, they are flogged for preaching—back down. But suddenly they start rejoicing even in their suffering and return to preaching—back up.

That's all in just one chapter. There are 28 chapters in the book of Acts!

The Christian life looks a lot like that. Some days it's up, other days it's down. There are constant battles but promised victories. However, when you fail to understand that, it is easy to grow bitter as things begin to go down. Or even when you are on the up, you might become pessimistic, assuming everything is going to go right back down. Thankfully, the Bible tells us what attitude we ought to have during the hills and the valleys. There is a verse I have held onto many times from the book of Ecclesiastes:

> In the day of prosperity be happy, but in the day of adversity consider—God has made the one as well as the other. (Ecclesiastes 7:14 NASB)

In other words, be happy when things are going great. Enjoy it, and keep moving forward. Thank God for what He has done today. But when you find yourself in a battle, consider the question: What is God doing through this?

On this rollercoaster Christian journey, it is important to make sure that you are sitting next to the right person. You don't want to be stuck next to someone who is ready to jump off as soon as the ride goes down. You want to be around people who will trust God no matter which way it's going. After all, attitudes can be infectious. I've been around people who try to become thermostats in the room. If they're happy, we all get to be happy, but if they're upset, everyone has to walk on eggshells. I want to journey with people who are going to rejoice on the way up and on the way down.

Before the Children of Israel could go into the Promised Land, they had to clear out a number of people from among them. In a sense, they were checking who they were sitting next to on the rollercoaster, fully aware that attitudes can be infectious. This is what the army command said in Deuteronomy:

> When you prepare for battle, the priest must come forward to speak to the troops. He will say to them, 'Listen to me, all you men of Israel! Do not be afraid as you go out to fight your enemies today! Do not lose heart or panic or tremble before them. For the Lord your God is going with you! He will fight for you against your enemies, and he will give you victory!' (Deuteronomy 20:2–4 NLT)

Then the process of subtraction begins:

> Then the officers of the army must address the troops and say, "Has anyone here just built a new house but not yet dedicated it? If so, you may go home! You might be killed in the battle, and someone else would dedicate your house. Has anyone here just planted a vineyard but not yet eaten any of its fruit? If so, you may go home! You might die in battle, and someone else would eat the first fruit. Has anyone here just become engaged to a woman but not yet married her? Well, you may go home and get married! You might die in the battle, and someone else would marry her." (Deuteronomy 20:5–7 NLT)

And finally comes this command:

> Is there a man here who is wavering in resolve and afraid? Let him go home right now so that he doesn't infect his fellows with his timidity and cowardly spirit. (Deuteronomy 20:8 MSG)

In other words, get rid of anyone who is not in this for the long haul, for those attitudes can spread quickly—particularly if you're in a fight!

Thankfully, they didn't need to do this by Acts 5, for the apostles were "all in" on that rollercoaster, willing to stay through both the ups and the downs. No one got off the ride. Notice that the entire chapter uses a group name that included all of them: the apostles. Here is how they are described throughout the chapter:

the apostles (verse 18)
they (verse 19)
them (verse 20)
them (verse 22)
the men (verse 25)
them (verse 26)
them (verse 27)
Peter and the apostles answered (verse 29)
them (verse 33)
the apostles (verse 40)
they (verse 41)
they (verse 42)

Nobody got off the ride! All of them agreed, "Up or down, we're going all the way with Jesus!"

The Bible tells us that after the Ananias and Sapphira incident, miraculous healings were taking place and the church began to grow.

> Also the people from the cities in the vicinity of Jerusalem were coming together, bringing people who were sick or afflicted with unclean spirits, and they were all being healed. But the high priest rose up, along with all his associates (that is the sect of the Sadducees), and they were filled with jealousy. They laid hands on the apostles and put them in a public jail. But during the night an angel of the Lord opened the gates of the prison, and taking them out he said, "Go, stand and speak to the people in the temple the whole message of this Life." Upon hearing this, they entered into the temple about daybreak and began to

> teach. Now when the high priest and his associates came, they called the Council together, even all the Senate of the sons of Israel, and sent orders to the prison house for them to be brought. But the officers who came did not find them in the prison; and they returned and reported back, saying, "We found the prison house locked quite securely and the guards standing at the doors; but when we had opened up, we found no one inside." (Acts 5:16–23 NASB)

I find it ironic that God used an angel to set them free because the Sadducees actually denied the existence of angels (see Acts 23:8). I can picture the apostles standing before them in court and the Sadducees asking, "How did you get out?"

"Duh, angels—which you don't believe in—set us free from jail!"

I want you to notice what the angel of the Lord said as he released them from prison, for I believe it pertains to us today. He said, "Go, stand and speak to the people in the temple" (verse 20). This is what comes after freedom. You and I haven't been set free just so we can be comfortable; we have been set free from sin so that we can do what God has called us to do: Go, stand, and speak. Each of those words carries a challenge for us today.

1. GO: THAT'S FAITH.

The first instruction is to go, and that takes faith. It is interesting that the first word from the angel of the Lord was also the first word of the Great Commission:

> Go therefore and make disciples of all the nations, baptizing them in the name of the Father and of the Son and of the Holy Spirit. (Matthew 28:19 NKJV)

Go is faith—stepping out onto thin ice. It's going where you've never been before. For the apostles, it was the temple. After the middle-of-the-night miracle, the release from jail was so that they would go to a certain public place, regardless of what anybody else told them to do.

I heard someone once say, “Everything you want and everything you don't have is outside of your comfort zone.” A few weeks ago, I was leaving the gym and had just said goodbye to the guy I'd been witnessing to. I was already out the door when the Holy Spirit said, “Go back and check on him. Let him know you care about him.”

“I'm already cleaned up and out,” I silently protested. “I’m sure he's fine.” But at that moment I felt God was interfering with my schedule, and I knew I needed to respond. I literally turned around and went back to ask the guy, “How are you doing? Talk to me.” He told me we need to talk, so we ended up setting up a time to have coffee. There are moments when God will pull you out of your comfort zone and tell you to go. Go involves movement. It will be uncomfortable, and you may feel like you're on thin ice, but when God instructs us to go, we are to obey.

Not long after 9/11 here in New York City, I was asked to do a funeral in Queens, New York, for a relative who was a fireman. It was my first time doing a relative's funeral, and I knew there would be a lot of firemen attending who had been on the scene during 9/11. I felt that “go” from the Lord, telling me that this was an opportunity to make plain the gospel of Jesus Christ. These men and women had basically seen hell and the results of evil. They needed to hear the good news of what Jesus had for their lives.

I'll never forget getting ready to step out of my comfort zone in that funeral home filled with men in uniform. The Holy Spirit told me, “You take them from beginning to end and share the gospel.” I admit, I was afraid, but as I stood there on what felt like thin ice, I went from Genesis to Revelation. I shared about the fall of man and ended with the flames of hell, telling them that there wasn't a fire hydrant in New York City able to douse those flames. But I explained that there was One who can, and it happened at the cross when the blood of Jesus dropped upon the flames of hell. I assured them that no matter what they had done, no matter what they had seen or experienced, they could be set free by the power of Jesus Christ.

I felt strongly that the Holy Spirit wanted me to invite them to raise their hands in response. In that funeral home, I watched as dozens upon dozens of New York's bravest raised their hands to receive Jesus Christ. As I was leaving, one of my relatives gave me his New York City Fire Department jacket—the one he wore as he was digging through the rubble of the Twin Towers. I treasure that jacket; it's still in my closet to this day. In fact, I wore that jacket the very next day. It was hot, and I was sweating, but I was determined to wear it with pride. I walked through LaGuardia Airport and sat on the plane, dripping in sweat. The guy next to me asked, "Are you a fireman?"

"Yes I am," I said. "I put out the fires of hell." And I took that man from Genesis to Revelation and told him that God could touch him right at that moment on that Delta flight!

Sometimes you need to get out of your comfort zone. When you obey the "go," God goes with you. Go into the conversation, go to the family dinner that you've been avoiding, go get a cup of coffee with that person who is going to push your buttons. Who knows what God can do?

2. STAND: THAT'S AUTHORITY.

After you go, the next thing you need to do is stand. A few weeks ago, Ricardo and I led a chapel for a professional sports team. Whenever I speak to athletes or business people, I do two things: One, I bring a physical black Bible so there is no mistake about where my message is coming from. I do this because Isaiah 55:11 says, "His word shall not return void." If I preach the Word, it doesn't come back void. Two, I will lift up the name of Jesus. Jesus says in John 12:32, "If I be lifted up, I will draw all men unto Me." I know that if I lift up the name of Jesus, there is something from heaven that draws them to God. Those are the promises I stand on, especially when speaking to athletes or business people.

I remember telling a chaplain, "I'm not a motivational speaker. I'm not going to tell you how to win. I'm not going speak about David and Goliath and tell you that you're David and that's Goliath and that you're going to win and go to the championship. I am here to share the truths of the Bible." That was my mandate from God.

Likewise, when the apostles were released from prison, they went to the temple and stood unashamed. They did exactly what they were asked to do, fully aware that they were operating under heaven's mandate. They understood that the authority of God, which instructed them to speak, was greater than the human authorities who told them not to. In the temple, they preached boldly. We don't know the immediate results, but we do know that it led to an opportunity for God to open another door for them:

> When they had brought them, they stood them before the Council. The high priest questioned them, saying, "We gave you strict orders not to continue teaching in this name, and yet, you have filled Jerusalem with your teaching and intend to bring this man's blood upon us." (Acts 5:27–28 NASB)

The Council that they stood before was the Sanhedrin—the Jewish high court of the time. It consisted of 71 members of priests, elders, and scribes, all of whom were responsible for the religious, judicial, and political functions of the Jews. These were the 71 most powerful people in all of Jerusalem, most of whom were Sadducees. And

God essentially said, "Watch Me open up the doors. You just go and stand."

After the high priest opened the proceedings by reminding everyone how the apostles were strictly ordered not to continue teaching in the name of Jesus, Peter boldly declared:

> We must obey God rather than men. (Acts 5:29 NASB)

There must be no compromise on this. Sometimes we hear the voice of the Sadducees telling us, "You can't preach; you can't witness here." Oftentimes the Sadducees are merely inside of our heads. "Don't pray for the sick. There's no hope. Nothing is going to happen." But that's when you have to say, "I must obey God rather than men."

Go: That's faith. Stand: That's authority. And finally, we are called to speak.

3. SPEAK: THAT'S BOLDNESS.

In order to stand, you must have authority. The Word of God is our authority to speak; it's where we find our boldness.

Last week, my family and I had some time off, so I went to Barnes and Noble on Fifth Avenue to get a book for vacation. While I was in the religious section, pulling out a book by C.S. Lewis, another individual was pulling out a book called *Queer Christians*. I began to think to myself, "How do I start a conversation here?"

Just as Peter spoke out without any preparation, I found myself with no preparation in Barnes and Noble. There are times when you just get thrown into the deep end, and all you can do is pray, "God, give me the right words!" Here is the verse I hold onto in those situations:

> I am the Lord your God, who brought you up out of Egypt.

> Open wide your mouth and I will fill it. (Psalm 81:10 NIV)

I once attended a rehearsal of some musicians, and before I knew it, I was blindsided. One of the musicians pulled me aside and said, "I know we preach the gospel here at this church, and we want people to be born again. But what about people in other countries who have never heard the gospel?"

It can be easy to let fear set in and say, "I'll get back to you," so that you can have time to Google the answer. But what should we do in those moments? We can't script what is going to happen tomorrow. What if someone sitting next to you on the train or in a waiting room sees your Bible and asks, "Why do you believe?" You can't say, "Oh, no. Don't ask me now. I'll meet you right here in the same place next Sunday with an answer." In those moments, we must open our mouth and believe God will fill it.

I looked at that individual and said, "Let me give you three verses regarding those who have never heard the gospel." And as I opened my mouth, God just kept giving me the words to say. "First, I want to give you a verse about creation:

> The heavens are telling the glory of God; they are a marvelous display of his craftsmanship. Day and night they keep on telling about God. Without a sound or word, silent in the skies, their message reaches out to all the world. The sun lives in the heavens where God placed it. (Psalm 19:1–4 TLB)

"So one, God's design is seen everywhere. Whether you're in Uganda or the Bronx, God shows up every single day at every single sunrise. And now here is a word about humanity:

> But God shows his anger from heaven against all sinful, evil men who push away the truth from them. For the

> truth about God is known to them instinctively; God has put this knowledge in their hearts. Since earliest times men have seen the earth and sky and all God made, and have known of his existence and great eternal power. So they will have no excuse when they stand before God at Judgment Day. Yes, they knew about him all right, but they wouldn't admit it or worship him or even thank him for all his daily care. And after a while they began to think up silly ideas of what God was like and what he wanted them to do. The result was that their foolish minds became dark and confused. (Romans 1:18–21 TLB)

"Paul says God has given everybody two witnesses—external and internal. Creation speaks about God; conscious also speaks about God. That is very clear. What is unclear is if a man has only these two witnesses, then how much is enough? I don't know. I do believe many people in first world countries who have heard this gospel will be judged more severely."

I then gave him one final verse, this time about God.

> Shall not the Judge of all the earth do right? (Genesis 18:25 NKJV)

"From conscious and creation, how much they know about God, I can't tell you. But what I do know is this: God is the judge, and He will do what is right. God does His job revealing Himself. Men will blame God, but God says truth is accessible, and He will rightly judge."

Even though I was unprepared for the question, when I simply opened my mouth, God was faithful to fill it.

Let's look at what happened when Peter opened up his mouth before the Sanhedrin. He ended up spontaneously preaching a powerful sermon:

> The God of our fathers raised up Jesus, whom you had put to death by hanging Him on a cross. He is the one whom God exalted to His right hand as a Prince and a Savior, to grant repentance to Israel, and forgiveness of sins. And we are witnesses of these things; and so is the Holy Spirit, whom God has given to those who obey Him. (Acts 5:30–32 NASB)

God gave Peter four sledgehammer thoughts to his sermon. One, there is a God to be obeyed. Two, there is a Savior who died for our sins. Three, forgiveness is available to anyone who asks. And four, you can receive power to live a victorious life, and He is the Holy Spirit. That was Peter's message.

> But when they heard this, they were cut to the quick and intended to kill them. (Acts 5:33 NASB)

It wasn't exactly a great altar call moment. I make no promises of how people will respond to your message. All I know is that our job is to go, stand, and speak. The Sanhedrin was eventually convinced not to kill the apostles when a man named Gamaliel warned that they might be fighting against God.

> They took his advice; and after calling the apostles in, they flogged them and ordered them not to speak in the name of Jesus, and then released them. (Acts 5:40 NASB)

Instead of killing the apostles, they flogged them. This word flogging is insightful. Flogging was a form of public shaming, with the intent of making an example out of the one being punished. The person would be stripped and given a maximum of 39 lashes in a public setting.

Standing up for truth at your workplace, in a science class at university, or at public school may result in "flogging" today. You may be publicly shamed. If you don't want to be flogged, you might want to get off this rollercoaster quickly because I believe it is coming! But we can be encouraged when we see what happened after the apostles were flogged:

> They went on their way from the presence of the Council, rejoicing that they had been considered worthy to suffer shame for His name. And every day, in the temple and from house to house, they kept right on teaching and preaching Jesus as the Christ. (Acts 5:41–42 NASB)

We know how to rejoice to music and answered prayers. However, we don't know how to rejoice when persecution comes. Churches in parts of the Middle East and Asia or in other countries where Christians are persecuted know a deep joy that we don't know in our country. There is a depth of rejoicing when you suffer for His name's sake that we have yet to experience. But get ready. Of course, I'm not wanting to get beat up, but I'm not backing down either.

Other than the threat of persecution, I believe what often holds us back from obeying the call to "go, stand, and speak" is the fear of man—in other words, we are afraid of losing our reputation. We don't want to be labeled as "religious." Yet consider God's words through the prophet Isaiah:

> I, I'm the One comforting you. What are you afraid of—or who? Some man or woman who'll soon be dead? Some poor wretch destined for dust? You've forgotten me, God, who made you, who unfurled the skies, who founded the earth. And here you are, quaking like a fragile tree before the tantrums of a tyrant who thinks he can kick down the world. But what will come of the tantrums? The victims will be released before you know it. They're not going to

> die. They're not even going to go hungry. For I am God, your very own God, who stirs up the sea and whips up the waves, named God-of-the-Angel-Armies. I teach you how to talk, word by word, and personally watch over you, even while I'm unfurling the skies, setting earth on solid foundations, and greeting Zion: 'Welcome, my people!'" So wake up! Rub the sleep from your eyes! Up on your feet. (Isaiah 51:12–17 MSG)

When we truly acknowledge who God is, we become willing to "go, stand, and speak," just as the apostles did. Fear of man begins to lose its grip. There comes a point when we must decide, "Who cares what people think? They didn't save me. They haven't provided for me. They didn't heal me. They can't change me. And they can't silence me!" Let's obey His call—stepping out in faith, authority, and boldness that comes from God Himself.

JUST TELL YOUR STORY: THE POWER OF A TESTIMONY

A little over 20 years ago, I had the privilege of traveling with some pastors to Rwanda, which is known as the Switzerland of Africa. The country is surrounded by a beautiful, mountainous landscape. The people we met were so amazing and kind, making it hard to imagine that just a little over ten years prior to our visit, the country had experienced a massive genocide.

Spanning a hundred days from April to July 1994, the members of the Tutsi ethnic group were being systematically eliminated by the Hutu militia, resulting in almost a million lives lost. We traveled with leaders from a Christian organization called Compassion International to visit feeding sites where hundreds of Tutsi children were executed. I found the Rwanda Holocaust Museum to be just as sobering as the Jewish Holocaust Museum. I heard countless stories from directors, families, and leaders who were all affected by this tragedy. However, the experience that left an indelible mark on my soul took place at a Sunday morning church service in Kigali, the capital of Rwanda.

I had asked one of the pastors traveling with our team to preach that Sunday. I just wanted to sit in the audience, and I am so happy that I did. What I experienced turned out to be far more significant than standing behind a pulpit.

Sitting in the congregation that Sunday, I watched a man in front of me who was so focused on Christ that he was just beaming with joy. His arms were lifted at every single song. He would clap constantly in worship; nothing around him seemed to matter. This man was missing both of his hands, yet he clapped with those nubs like no one I had ever seen. I was determined to know his story.

I later learned he was a Tutsi, and the penalty for being the "wrong" race during those hundred days was to have his hands held on a chopping block and cut off. And now this man was in front of me, clapping joyfully with no hands. It was a muted sound with those nubs, but I believe every time he clapped, in heaven it resounded loudly. That man worshipped with no animosity in a place where other ethnic groups were gathered, including Hutus—the people responsible for killing his family. Yet this man had his eyes fixed on heaven. He had forgiven his enemies and worshiped God with fervency. I was deeply impacted as I watched this man who did so much with the little that he had.

After church, I talked with him and hugged him. I even took both of those nubs and kissed them. I said to him, "I want you to lay your hands on me and pray for me." And at that moment, over 20 years ago, I thought to myself, "If he can worship with excitement and fervor with no hands, what am I doing with two hands? If a man who lost his loved ones in a genocide has been able to forgive and move on, why am I holding onto offense? God has given me two good hands. My pain is nowhere near this man's, yet here I am, holding back when so much more has been given to me."

I determined in my heart at that point, "I will forgive fast. I will not be ashamed of this gospel. I will not be offended by petty arguments or people who have hurt me. I will not be lukewarm when it comes to worship, the Word, and loving God. I will not be disobedient. I will not hold on to unforgiveness. I will be a disciple in love with Jesus

Christ. I will be a fervent worshiper who gives God every part of me. I will always sing. I will always worship. I will always tell my story."

Now whenever I don't feel like telling my story, I think about the church service in Rwanda. It reminds me that each of us has a story worth telling. Through our stories, others see the faithfulness of God. Although not many of us have been through a genocide, all of our God stories involve moments when we found ourselves in a low place—at rock bottom. There is a powerful verse in the Bible that calls it the "great deep."

> Was it not You who dried up the sea, the waters of the great deep; who made the depths of the sea a pathway for the redeemed to cross over? (Isaiah 51:10 NASB)

I love the way The Message version puts it:

> . . . and then made the bottom of the ocean a road for the redeemed. (Isaiah 51:10 MSG)

He makes the great deep into a path for the redeemed! God is telling us that He can take the worst of the worst and make it a path to the best and to freedom.

When I was in Detroit in the 1980s, we would hand tracts, which were gospel booklets, out on the streets. One of my favorites was called *Rock Bottom* by David Wilkerson. I used to hold onto dozens of them and hand them out to people. It was written for those who hit the "great deep"—the lowest part of life where the next step lower was literally hell for them. I would ask, "Have you hit rock bottom? Are you ready for a new life?" I knew that where they were was actually a path to get them to the other side. Like Isaiah 51:10 says, the lowest place had the potential to becomc a road to their miracle.

When you hit your lowest point, whether you are unsaved or saved, it is amazing how God will use the road of the great deep to bring you to Himself. It is in those depths that we become aware of our need of God. The depths become a pathway back to where we belong, and the pathway always has a story. You need to tell that story wherever you go.

Look at how Peter exalts those who have traveled from the rock bottom to the other side.

> But you are the ones chosen by God, chosen for the high calling of priestly work, chosen to be a holy people, God's instruments to do his work and speak out for him, to tell others of the night-and-day difference he made for you—from nothing to something, from rejected to accepted. (1 Peter 2:9–10 MSG)

Just tell your story! Tell others of your night-and-day story, the difference God made in changing you from nothing to something, from rejected to accepted. There is power in your testimony. When you tell your story, here are five things I want you to remember:

1. PEOPLE SHOULD PRAISE GOD, NOT YOU

When you tell your story, it becomes a true testimony when they praise God, not you. Throughout the letters of the New Testament, Paul would constantly tell his rock-bottom, depths-of-the-ocean story. In fact, he told it for decades. Here is one of those moments when he shared his testimony:

> By now you have heard stories of how severely I harassed and persecuted Christians and did my best to systematically destroy God's church, all because of my radical devotion to the Jewish religion. My zeal and passion for the doctrines of Judaism distinguished me among my people, for I was far more advanced in my religious instruction than others my age. But then God called me by his grace; and in love,

> he chose me from my birth to be his. God's grace unveiled his Son in me so that I would proclaim him to the non-Jewish people of the world. After I had this encounter I kept it a secret for some time, sharing it with no one. And I chose not to run to Jerusalem to try to impress those who had become apostles before me. Instead, I went away into the Arabian Desert for a season until I returned to Damascus, where I had first encountered Jesus. I remained there for three years until I eventually went up to Jerusalem and met the apostle Peter and stayed with him for a couple of weeks so I could get to know him better. The only other apostle I met during that time was James, the Lord's brother. Everything I'm describing to you I confess before God is the absolute truth. After my stay in Jerusalem, I went to Syria and southeast Turkey, but remained unknown to the Jewish believers in Judea. (Galatians 1:13–21 TPT)

A biography always ends with a person—their story and their accomplishments. But a testimony is different. A testimony ends with what God did. A person is the star of the biography; God is the star of a testimony. Paul didn't share his biography. He shared his testimony and gave all the glory to God. He even pointed out how people recognized that what happened to him couldn't have happened unless God had stepped in:

> The only thing they heard about me was this: "Our former enemy, who once brutally persecuted us, is now preaching the good news of the faith that he was once obsessed with destroying!" Because of the transformation that took place in my life, they praised God even more! (Galatians 1:23–24 TPT)

The transformation that took place in his life was miraculous.

Someone once said it like this: "God formed man. Sin deformed him. Education informs him. Religion may reform him. But only Jesus Christ can transform him." Don't stop at education. Don't stop at a PhD; keep moving on. And for heaven's sake, don't stop at religion. Go all the way. Let the transforming work of Jesus take place in your life. When he was Saul, he went from education and even into religion, but his life wasn't transformed until he encountered Jesus Christ. By the time he told his story, people were drawn to God, not to Paul. That is the mark of a powerful testimony.

The following powerful testimony was recently sent in from somebody who is now serving with our online team:

> When I was a child, my mother died, and the brokenness shaped my life and the image I had of myself. But God didn't leave me behind. I was confronted with His love and plan for my life. A few years later, as a young child, I went to a Billy Graham crusade and heard of the love of Jesus—that He would offer forgiveness. I went to the altar and gave my life to Christ. My decision was sincere, but what happened next was catastrophic. My sister and I were sexually abused by a close member of our family. I spent the next several years spiraling into a self-destructive lifestyle that included an abusive marriage.
>
> Drug abuse led to a life of crime, though I never forgot the message I heard about Jesus. And God was about to intervene just like He did for Paul on the road to Damascus. His actions led me to Times Square Church through some unexpected, unusual ways. I used to do drug deals in the streets. I used a public payphone on the sidewalk where I dealt so I wouldn't get caught. One day I saw something in the phone booth and picked it up. It was a David Wilkerson sermon letter which intrigued me,

so I read it and started to follow TSC online and David Wilkerson's website. For years, I was still struggling with personal issues and a criminal lifestyle. Then in 1994, I went to jail, and this time I went to jail for something I didn't do. I've done plenty of wrong things, but this time I was really innocent.

I was incarcerated, and in my cell, I discovered a surprise under my mattress. It was David Wilkerson's book *Set the Trumpet to Thy Mouth*. There's no doubt that God was getting my attention! One night God came in a dream, asked me to not fight the prison sentence, and to do the full time I was facing. If you think this was shocking to me, you should have seen the court's reaction. I served the full sentence, but while in prison I met a woman named Brenda who taught Bible studies. She became a spiritual mother to me. It was no coincidence that many of her teachings were by this man of God that I kept discovering through his newsletter and book. Those messages in the Bible studies began to deal with my hard heart. I was so lost, but over time, the reality of how faithful God had been sunk in. During those years that I asked for full incarceration, He saved my life. He spared me some bad potential outcomes if I would've left.

In 1996, I was released from prison, a different woman—free from drug addiction with the knowledge that Jesus really does love me. I stayed connected with Times Square Church, continuing to follow Brother Dave and Carter Conlon and now Tim Dilena. The church has remained an important part of my life and that of my family as they dealt with their own struggles.

I've been blessed to have served. I serve with the online

> team. Right now, I'm active in supporting other believers in the chats that we have for our live stream services. I'm so thankful for Times Square Church with life-changing messages that have taken me deeper into my relationship with God. I am saved. I thank God for His mercy. I thank God for His grace.

When I hear those kinds of stories, I don't praise her; I praise God. It's the miraculous power of God that changed her life!

2. TESTIMONIES CRUSH THE ENEMY'S LIES

Something powerful happens when people tell their testimonies. In fact, the Bible says that these testimonies have devil-defeating power.

> They overcame him by the blood of the Lamb, and by the word of their testimony. (Revelation 12:11 KJV)

The "him" they overcame is Satan. The apostle John makes a profound statement when he says that our testimony is right underneath the power of the blood of Jesus. We plead the blood of Jesus, we share our testimony, people glorify God, and the devil is defeated! Your testimony has Satan-defeating power.

I have witnessed the power of the testimony many times—particularly over the devil's number one weapon: his lies. When I was 19 years old and handing out those tracts in Detroit, they ended up putting me in a prostitution hotel to lead a Bible study. That is where I learned how to preach—in front of pimps and prostitutes. Every Thursday night for five years, I would go down there and preach at 7:05 p.m. We didn't start at seven o'clock because that was when they would show the lottery numbers for the city. But at 7:05 p.m., people would be ready to come to this Bible study with their stolen Gideon Bibles. We would have pimps, prostitutes, drug addicts, and alcoholics.

God will often save the worst first and deal with the enemy's lies by having people witness miraculously changed lives. We saw it again when we took over the triple-X theater in Detroit and turned it into a church. The first person God saved was Kimutchi, the theater's prostitute. It was a demonstration to all the other prostitutes in the area that God can set them free as well. Testimonies crush the lies of the enemy that say "God doesn't love you" or "God can't change you." When people see a life transformed by Jesus, it is undeniable proof that He still saves!

3. TESTIMONIES SILENCE THE CRITICS AND MAKE US GET LOUDER

It has been said that a man with an experience is never at the mercy of a man with an argument. That means a profound spiritual experience will not be swayed by intellectual or even theological arguments. It is hard to convince me that God doesn't exist when so many miracles are happening in people's lives.

Recently, during a Sunday morning service, our church joined in prayer for a family in the Netherlands. Live on the screen, we saw the father dedicating his son in an Amsterdam hospital. This little boy was about to undergo a major operation for a rare and serious heart condition. Our church dedicated him to the Lord and then prayed for him. I received this text from the family the next day:

> The operation was successful! We are incredibly grateful to share that his surgery is complete—and it went "wonder goed," as the surgeon literally said in Dutch. (It went miraculously well!) We caught a brief glimpse of our son in the hallway of the ICU as they were settling him into his room. His chest is closed, and the recovery journey is now beginning. No arrhythmias occurred during the entire procedure. It was finished in under 4 hours—normal is 4–6 hours without complications. Thank you again for every

> prayer, every message, and every moment of support. God truly carried our son—and us—through today.

On the other side of Holland, the little boy's grandmother was in a different hospital with her body full of cancer. This woman and her husband were commissioned by David Wilkerson to start the first Teen Challenge in Amsterdam, making them the first Teen Challenge directors in Europe. Now she was battling cancer that was aggressively attacking her organs. We saw this precious woman on the screen as well, and we prayed for total healing. Here is the text I received a couple of days later:

> My mom began to gain strength, started eating again—and now, they're even expecting her to return home. That service was truly a turning point. Mom had three full meals today... hasn't happened for 8 days when she was barely eating. When I saw her Thursday, I thought it would be the last time.

After she had returned home a few days later, I received this update:

> Mom is still getting stronger. My parents went on a date last night!

God is still doing miracles today! The first recorded miracle after the birth of the church was the healing of a man who had been lame from birth (see Acts 3). This man was a fixture at the temple gate, begging for money. If you made plans to go to the 3 p.m. Jewish prayer meeting, this man would ask you for money at the gate called Beautiful. But a miracle happened the day after Pentecost. He asked for money as usual, but this time he asked Peter and John—who believed in a resurrected, miracle-working Jesus.

> He looked up, expecting to get something from them. Peter said, "I don't have a nickel to my name, but what I do

> have, I give you: In the name of Jesus Christ of Nazareth, walk!" He grabbed him by the right hand and pulled him up. In an instant his feet and ankles became firm. He jumped to his feet and walked. The man went into the Temple with them, walking back and forth, dancing and praising God. Everybody there saw him walking around and praising God. They recognized him as the one who sat begging at the Temple's Gate Beautiful and rubbed their eyes, astonished, scarcely believing what they were seeing. (Acts 3:5–10 MSG)

Instead of merely getting a few coins, this man ended up dancing and praising God! Of course, the greatest religious minds were upset with this miracle. Not only did all the people witness it, Peter ended up preaching after the miracle, and 5,000 people got saved (see Acts 4:4)! After the day of Pentecost, 3,000 got saved, and now after this miracle, 5,000 more were added to the church. That's the power of a testimony. It has the ability to silence the critics, but it opens the mouths of the Christians. After the miracle, Peter boldly declared:

> "Salvation comes no other way; no other name has been or will be given to us by which we can be saved, only this one." They couldn't take their eyes off them—Peter and John standing there so confident, so sure of themselves! Their fascination deepened when they realized these two were laymen with no training in Scripture or formal education. They recognized them as companions of Jesus. But with the man right before them, seeing him standing there so upright—so healed!—what could they say against that? (Acts 4:12–14 MSG)

What can you say when there is a guy dancing and praising the Lord? Suddenly the mouths of the critics had nothing left to say, while the church was going, "How can we be quiet?" Even when the religious leaders had forbidden them from speaking or teaching in the name of Jesus, Peter and John replied:

> Whether it's right in God's eyes to listen to you rather than to God, you decide. As for us, there's no question—we can't keep quiet about what we've seen and heard. (Acts 4:19–20 MSG)

The critics couldn't speak, and the church couldn't keep quiet!

4. TESTIMONIES HAVE NO EXPIRATION DATE

Some people find themselves at a loss for words when they are trying to witness to others. Here's what to do in those situations: Just tell your story. Tell them how God brought you from darkness to light.

We already read Paul's testimony in the first chapter of Galatians. Paul tells his story in both Acts 22 and Acts 26 as well. In Acts 22, standing before a hostile crowd in Jerusalem that intended to kill him, Paul tells them his conversion story. In Acts 26, he was brought before the most powerful people—the governor and the king. What does he say to them? He tells his story again. Paul keeps telling his conversion story.

I want you to take note of the following dates. Paul became a Christian in Acts 9, which is 34 AD. Paul tells his testimony in Acts 22, in 59 AD. Paul then tells his testimony again in Acts 26, in 62 AD. That means Paul was still telling his testimony 25 and 28 years later! Don't ever think you can't keep telling your story.

Here is his testimony speech in Acts 26.

> I used to believe that I ought to do everything I could to oppose the very name of Jesus the Nazarene. Indeed, I did just that in Jerusalem. Authorized by the leading priests, I caused many believers there to be sent to prison. And I

> cast my vote against them when they were condemned to death. Many times I had them punished in the synagogues to get them to curse Jesus. I was so violently opposed to them that I even chased them down in foreign cities. One day I was on such a mission to Damascus, armed with the authority and commission of the leading priests. About noon, Your Majesty, as I was on the road, a light from heaven brighter than the sun shone down on me and my companions. We all fell down, and I heard a voice saying to me in Aramaic, "Saul, Saul, why are you persecuting me? It is useless for you to fight against my will."
>
> "Who are you, lord?" I asked.
>
> And the Lord replied, "I am Jesus, the one you are persecuting. Now get to your feet! For I have appeared to you to appoint you as my servant and witness. Tell people that you have seen me, and tell them what I will show you in the future. And I will rescue you from both your own people and the Gentiles. Yes, I am sending you to the Gentiles to open their eyes, so they may turn from darkness to light and from the power of Satan to God. Then they will receive forgiveness for their sins and be given a place among God's people, who are set apart by faith in me." (Acts 26:9–18 NLT)

When you are engaged in a talk and suddenly don't know what to say, just tell them your story. Paul told his story to an angry mob and then again a few years later to the highest officials.

Last month, while I was in Greece for a pastor's conference, I had the opportunity to listen to a testimony that is 70 years old. That night, I heard Nicky Cruz tell his story once again. He spoke about how he was regularly beaten from age three and a half all the way up to age nine in Puerto Rico. His own father called him "a son of Satan." At 15, Nicky was sent to New York, where he got involved with gangs, drugs, and violence—until a Pennsylvania preacher showed up in Brooklyn and told him about Jesus. In 1958, at the St. Nicholas Arena in Manhattan, Nicky Cruz—the feared warlord—gave his heart to the Lord. He was 17 years old when he got saved. And now at 87 years old, when he tells his story, it sounds as if he was in the gangs just last week. I watched Nicky tell that testimony with no expiration date—as fresh as it was when he told it decades before. He has spoken that testimony to over 50 million people. All he does is tell his story, and millions have come to Christ.

I am presently reading a biography about D. L. Moody, who was considered the greatest American evangelist until Billy Graham came on the scene. They estimate that Moody has personally led a million people to the Lord. In his biography, he tells of a time when he had just finished a meeting, speaking to people to give their heart to Christ. He was sharing testimonies, and some religious woman came up to him and said, "Moody, I heard those stories before." This was his response: "I must tell those stories over and over again."[49] Who cares what a religious lady is saying? I have heard Nicky's testimony a hundred times. And every time I hear it, my heart is challenged.

5. IT'S SIMPLE, DON'T COMPLICATE IT

Shannon L. Alder once said, "God can deliver you so well that some people won't believe your testimony."[50] That is the power of God. It is what happens when the greatest power in the universe collides with our powerless lives. People want to complicate it, but it is really quite simple.

It is amazing that when Jesus healed a blind man who was a beggar, somehow no one could believe it.

> His neighbors and others who knew him as a blind beggar asked each other, "Isn't this the man who used to sit and beg?" Some said he was, and others said, "No, he just looks like him!" But the beggar kept saying, "Yes, I am the same one!" (John 9:8–9 NLT)

When you tell your story, don't be surprised if not everyone believes and accepts it. When my wife got saved, there were people in her life who thought she was in a cult.

In the end, the man who received the miracle had to spell it out plainly for everyone:

> One thing I do know. I was blind but now I see! (John 9:25 NIV)

It was simple: I was blind, but now I see. Now I see things differently, I see people differently, I see God differently. My eyes have been opened to see what I could not see before.

Over the years, I have heard people say, "I don't have a good testimony." I don't have a Nicky Cruz testimony either. I was born and raised in church, and I am thankful for that. I have never had an addiction, and I don't apologize for that testimony. But here is what we need to understand: Many people assume they don't have a testimony because they don't have a dramatic story of going from bad to good. That might seem true, but that's not the gospel. Leonard Ravenhill said it like this: "Jesus didn't come into the world to make bad men good. He came into the world to make dead men live."[51] We were all dead without Jesus. That means you are a living testimony of God's resurrection power—bringing you from death to life. It's that simple. I used to wonder, "God, why would You put me in a prostitution hotel to preach for five years? Why would You let me pastor in what used to be a triple-X theater? I was born in the church. I'm a good guy. I don't have a past like that. You should send someone else, not me."

But that is what God does. It's not about us going from bad to good, it's about how we all went from death to life. God is not trying to make bad people good. Many will argue that they are not that bad of a person. They won't give their heart to God because they are relying upon their own good works. They give money to charity. They don't hurt puppies. Great, but it doesn't change things because the issue is not about going from bad to good. The problem is that without Christ, we are all dead, and our good works mean nothing. We must go from death to life. That is what Jesus came to do. It's that simple. I was blind, but now I see. I was dead, but now I'm alive. That means we all have a testimony—one that is worth sharing.

SPEAKING TO ETERNITY

Her name is iconic, especially among those who face physical challenges. Helen Keller was both blind and deaf, yet she overcame immense obstacles to learn how to communicate. Her story and accomplishments are nothing short of astounding. Anne Sullivan became Helen's teacher when Helen was five years old. Anne found a way to communicate with Helen by spelling words on her hand. She would spill water on her hand while spelling out the words to try to get her to communicate. The story is told that Anne attempted to explain God to this blind and deaf girl. She started to put symbols for God on her palm, and much to Anne's surprise, Helen spelled back on Anne's palm these words: "Thank you for telling me God's name, for He has touched me many times before. I knew He was there, I just didn't know His name."[52]

How did Helen already know God? As Anne was communicating this to Helen, instead of it being a discovery, it became confirmation of something that was already resident within her. It is called speaking to eternity. The richest man in the world, Solomon, discovered something about all humanity. In his writings in the book of Ecclesiastes, he reveals a sacred place in every man's heart:

He has put eternity into man's heart. (Ecclesiastes 3:11 ESV)

God has put eternity into every person's heart. It is both profound and sobering to realize that when you speak to someone, you are not just speaking to an individual but to an eternal being. C. S. Lewis reminds us with this incredible thought: "There are no ordinary people . . . It is immortals whom we joke with, work with, marry, snub, and exploit . . ."[53] Jesus is the Alpha and Omega, but you are Omega. You had a beginning, but you will have no end. When you speak to others, you are speaking to people who will live forever.

Only eternal language can reach the part of the heart that has eternity set in it. Much of today's current event witnessing and preaching is shallow and ineffective. We must speak what is eternal to truly reach souls.

I remember the first time this truth hit me like a sledgehammer. I was 19 years old and had just moved to Detroit. We had a house where we would bring young men off the streets—those who didn't quite need a program but were still struggling and needed discipleship.

Coming home one day from church, I realized that one of the guys in our house had stolen something from me. Over the course of my life and ministry, I have had many things stolen. One time someone broke into my car and took all my Christian cassette tapes and my Bible. At least it was a Christian thief. But this time someone had stolen my JVC stereo. We called it a boombox. I had received it as a high school graduation gift. I'll never forget when I asked my parents for it. It was like asking for a car because it cost over $300, which they thought was outrageous, but they still got it for me. I loved that JVC boombox and took it with me to university. My dorm room was in the basement, and I would blast Christian music and David Wilkerson sermons on that boombox with my door open. People would stop by, and I considered it an evangelistic tool. But now one of the guys had stolen it and sold it at a pawn shop to get money for crack. I knew exactly who took it, and I was so upset. I remember sitting on the porch, waiting for him to come back from the job that we helped him get, back to the house that we provided.

When he returned, I knew at that point I was faced with a choice. I could speak out of my anger, or I could speak to eternity. I didn't know where the words came from except the Holy Spirit when I looked at him and said, "You got something that was very valuable to me, but you didn't get my treasure because I don't keep my treasures in this house." He stood there, dumbfounded. I continued, "Jesus said, 'Do not store up for yourself treasures on earth where moth and rust corrupt, where thieves break in and steal. For where your treasure is, there your heart will be also.'"

I remember looking at this young man who thought I was going to respond with anger and call the cops. Instead, I watched him respond to the eternal words I spoke. I wasn't speaking to the crime or what he had done; I was speaking to a spot in his heart. Everyone he had stolen from before spoke to his mind and spoke about consequences. But it was entirely different to have somebody speak to a spot in his heart that needed to be spoken to—a spot set there by God Himself.

A few weeks ago, we had a profound Tuesday night service as Will Bassett from England shared his testimony. I have been in the ministry for 42 years and have never seen anything like what we had that night. Will pastors in the area of what is considered one of the greatest universities in the world, Oxford University. He pastors a church, but he stutters. I don't remember ever listening to a stuttering pastor—until that night. Will spoke about how "weakness is the way." Most of us have thorns that others can't see. Will explained, "But my thorn is out there for everybody to see. That's why I have to trust God." To hear this man stutter with an anointing was like listening to Moses. Will sent me this message a few days later:

A few days before I preached, God put on my heart that I'd be speaking to a younger me in the audience—that I'd be speaking to a young man with a speech impediment who feels called to the ministry. So I began praying for that person as I was going to stand in this pulpit. After the service, I prayed with a number of people. Pastor Tim, just as I was about to leave, a young man, who we will call Trey, came up to me. He had a noticeable stutter as he talked to me and told me that God spoke to him through the message. He felt called to the ministry for some time but had put it off and thought he was not fit for ministry because he stuttered and had a speech impediment. Sarah and I prayed for him, and he said that night, because of that sermon, he's decided to answer the call and step into the role of youth pastor at his father's church. Praise God!

That night, Will spoke eternity into that boy's heart. He spoke about God's calling inside of him. Truth is the language of eternity; it is what that spot in the heart understands. David said it this way:

> The entirety of Your word is truth, and every one of Your righteous judgments endures forever. (Psalm 119:160 NKJV)

The Word of God is truth that endures forever because it has already been settled.

> Forever, O Lord, Your word is settled in heaven. (Psalm 119:89 NKJV)

The issue has been settled in heaven, not a court. God's Word never gets outdated; His truth endures forever. It never gets to be voted on or vetoed. As you speak to people, always bring the Word of God to bear on every heart. That is a sure way to speak to eternity—using an eternal language:

> Heaven and earth will pass away, but My words will not

pass away. (Matthew 24:35 NASB)

I was witnessing to a professional athlete for some time. His upbringing and worldview had him pretty set about God's Word—he wanted no part of it. I had never invited him to church, but I would always invite him to go out and talk one-on-one. I wanted him to have time when I could speak into his life instead of just sitting in an audience, listening to a message.

And then unexpectedly, without any invitation from me, he showed up at church one night. It had to be God. When I stood at the pulpit and saw him there, my initial thought was, "Oh no, this is the wrong night for him to show up." That night, I was planning to preach on eternal punishment and hell. I thought perhaps I had missed it and was scrambling through the Bible, thinking maybe God wanted me to speak on something else.

In the end, I reluctantly agreed to preach the message the Holy Spirit had given me. I was pretty sure our one-on-one conversations would be over. When I saw him after church, I was too embarrassed to ask, "So what did you think of the message?" Instead, I simply asked, "Hey, do you want to meet again?"

"Of course," he replied. And then I was even more surprised when he continued, "The message on hell made sense to me. If God exists, there has to be a place to punish sin and evil."

I couldn't believe it. But now I understand that the sermon was speaking to the eternity in his heart. Men come up with crazy doctrines like annihilationism that states that hell doesn't exist, hoping not to offend anybody. But when you do that, you never speak to the eternity that is in their heart—the forever part of their heart. You are trying hard not to offend, but avoiding offense is not what draws people to God. It is when people hear the truth of God's Word that things begin to make sense, because eternity in the heart understands eternal language.

A story is told about an elderly Jewish woman named Ellie who was speaking in a Tennessee congregation right outside of Nashville. She told the story about the great price that was paid for her to find Christ. She had been imprisoned in a concentration camp with no hope for survival, convinced that her only chance would be hinged on an escape. She meticulously made her plans, and on the night she broke for freedom, everything went well—until she had to scale the barbed wire fence in Auschwitz. She was halfway up the fence when she was spotted by a Nazi SS guard. At gunpoint, he screamed for her to stop. She fell to the ground, bleeding and weeping, her only hope vanished. But miraculously, the guard recognized her as a classmate from school. During their adolescent years they had been best friends, but now they were on opposite sides. He was German and she was a Jew.

Agonizing over her plight, Ellie cried out to her friend, "Rolfe, go ahead and kill me. I have no reason to live."

The guard replied, "Ellie, you're so wrong. There's everything to live for, as long as you know who to live for. I'm going to let you go and I'll guard you until you climb the wall and get on the other side. But you have to promise me one thing."

Ellie couldn't believe what was happening. In her disbelief, she asked, "What is it, Rolfe?"

He said, "Promise me when you get on the other side and are free, you will ask one question continuously until someone answers it: Why does Jesus Christ make life worth living? He is the only reason to live. Promise me you will ask until you get the answer."

Ellie shouted, "Yes, I promise!" as she scampered over the barbed wire. She ran for freedom and then heard several gunshots. She glanced over her shoulder to see if Rolfe had changed his mind and was now seeking to kill her. Instead, she saw his body dead on the ground. Another guard had shot him for treason. That hasty promise she made to gain freedom now took on new meaning.

"The young man gave his life so I could have a chance for freedom," Ellie told that Tennessee church. "I did exactly as Rolfe told me. I kept asking and asking until one day I met someone who answered the question. I am a Christian today because Rolfe sacrificed his life for me. May our witness for Christ be as valiant as that brave man's."

A Nazi concentration camp guard spoke to the eternity in the heart of that little Jewish girl, giving her a chance to live and find Christ. It is about speaking truth. When churches merely want to address every social issue, it is a dead end. The only thing that begins to speak to the heart, transcending even country lines, is the eternal Word of God.

Jesus essentially did the same thing to a rich young man that the Nazi guard did to Ellie. He spoke to eternity and offered him a choice. But instead of doing what Ellie did, this young man left Christ and walked away. We know him as the rich young ruler:

> As He was setting out on a journey, a man ran up to Him and knelt before Him, and asked Him, "Good Teacher, what shall I do to inherit eternal life?" And Jesus said to him, "Why do you call Me good? No one is good except God alone. You know the commandments, 'Do not murder, do not commit adultery, do not steal, do not bear false witness, do not defraud, honor your father and mother.'" And he said to Him, "Teacher, I have kept all these things from my youth up." Looking at him, Jesus felt a love for him and said to him, "One thing you lack: go and sell all you possess and give to the poor, and you will have treasure in

> heaven; and come, follow Me." But at these words he was saddened, and he went away grieving, for he was one who owned much property. (Mark 10:17–22 NASB)

This young man was rich, he ran and knelt before Jesus, and he was interested in spiritual things. I was thinking, "Jesus, make this one work. You won't have to worry about money for the ministry. No more offerings. This guy can bankroll you." I would have had him on his knees, praying a prayer to be born again. But Jesus messes the whole thing up. Instead of answering the question, "What shall I do to inherit eternal life?" Jesus asked a follow-up question: "Why do you call me good? Only God is good."

Why is this so huge? The young man calls Jesus good, and since God is the only one who is good, then Jesus is God. That means God is now speaking to him. So Jesus's follow-up question reveals whether this is just all talk or if this young man really does believe.

C. S. Lewis said it this way: "You never know how much you really believe anything until its truth or falsehood becomes a matter of life and death to you. It is easy to say you believe a rope to be strong and sound as long as you are merely using it to cord a box. But suppose you had to hang by that rope over a precipice. Wouldn't you then first discover how much you really trusted it?"[54]

Jesus was taking the rope off the box and hanging it over the cliff. That is where the young man's theology and belief fell apart. The bottom line was: Are you willing to do what God is asking you? This young man was willing to do as much as he could until Jesus interfered with his life and things became uncomfortable.

Jesus's question was about to intersect with eternity. When Jesus said "one thing you lack," He was not talking about living a life of abject poverty in order to follow Him, as some would try to build a doctrine around. The issue was bigger than that. This was about the question: Did you just call Me God? And if you are speaking with God right now, are you willing to agree with Him? It was all going great until the good teacher became God. Suddenly when God speaks, we have problems. The rich young man came with his own agenda and his own truth, and God was now interfering with his lifestyle. Everybody loves Jesus until He has something to say about their life. Everybody wants to be part of a church until God's Word speaks something contrary to how they are living. Suddenly they have to find a different church that will agree with their lifestyle. You might be able to find a church that agrees with you, but it is very dangerous. I don't want people agreeing with me. I want to agree with God.

When Jesus said, "Come, follow Me," many believe that this was a discipleship call, just like He extended to the 12. This young man was being called to something greater than he had ever known, but it would cost him everything—his own opinions and viewpoints. In the presence of God, everything must bow. Jesus was speaking to eternity. He was defining God, discussing eternal life, and distinguishing what true treasure really is. As His words hit the eternity in this young man's heart, he was left with no choice but to confront it. That is what speaking to eternity does—it exposes what truly matters and demands a response.

We see this again when Jesus was ending His Sermon on the Mount. He spoke to eternity and divided humanity into two groups—those on a wide road and those on a narrow road.

> You can enter God's Kingdom only through the narrow gate. The highway to hell is broad, and its gate is wide for the many who choose that way. But the gateway to life is very narrow and the road is difficult, and only a few ever find it. (Matthew 7:13–14 NLT)

Jesus was saying that all of humanity was born on the wide road. Nothing needs to be done by you or me to stay and live on this wide road. Yet Jesus warns us that the wide road leads to hell. The second road that leads to heaven is the narrow road. That road has a toll to get on it. A decision must be made to be born again.

C. S. Lewis finishes that thought with these words: "If I find in myself a desire which no experience in this world can satisfy, the most probable explanation is that I was made for another world."[55] When you have tried everything—that boyfriend, that girlfriend, excelling in sports, getting that dream job, moving to an ideal place—only to realize that it doesn't satisfy, here is the only explanation: I wasn't made for this world. I was made for eternity.

It is that spot called eternity in our hearts that nothing in this world can satisfy. And because God Himself set it in each of our hearts, we are capable of recognizing and responding to His eternal words. We may not always understand it, but something in us knows when truth is speaking.

I recently heard a remarkable story told by Dr. Ed Young, the pastor of Second Baptist Church of Houston, Texas. Israeli troops were doing relief work in Gaza, standing at a distance from the Palestinian people. Suddenly, out of nowhere, a King Charles Spaniel dog comes running out of the crowd toward the Jewish soldiers and jumped right into one of the soldier's arms. A King Charles Spaniel is the last thing you would expect in a war zone. It was so unusual that the soldiers kept the dog and brought it back to Jerusalem. They eventually discovered that the dog had a chip in it. His original owners, an Israeli man and his wife, had been taken as hostages and killed in Gaza, but their dog was kept alive. When the dog heard Hebrew being spoken, he broke rank and ran to those soldiers.[56] To this dog, that was home. As I heard this story, all I kept thinking about was this verse:

> My sheep recognize my voice. I know them, and they follow me. (John 10:27 MSG)

That is what speaking to eternity does. It calls to something deep within us—that part of our heart that God placed there. Eternity in the heart recognizes and responds to the sound of His voice. When people hear truth, something awakens, and they are drawn home. So let's speak to eternity, opening the way for people to hear God and follow Him.

15

LIGHT VERSUS LIGHTNING

A late British evangelist once reminded us not to forget about the "fifth gospel." Don't get nervous, I know that Matthew, Mark, Luke and John are the four gospels in the inspired Word of God. The fifth gospel, however, is also very important and cannot be overlooked. As Gypsy Smith said, "There are five Gospels: Matthew, Mark, Luke, John, and the Christian, but most people never read the first four."[57]

It is our lives that people are going to read. They spend a lot of time on our campuses, in our apartment buildings, and on our jobs, watching how we live. Charles Spurgeon once said it this way: "I would not give much for your religion unless it can be seen. Lamps do not talk, but they do shine."[58]

I have a friend who works in a very influential and visual industry. One day I asked him, "Do you know any serious believers in your industry?"

He told me, "There are many who openly profess to being a Christian, but they live their lives horribly." Wearing a Christian T-shirt yet having a foul mouth simply does not work. It is a contradiction. In fact, when a poll was taken of college students, asking: "What is the first thing that comes to mind when you hear the word Christianity?" the most common response was that Christians don't practice what they preach.[59]

Surveys conducted by the Barna Group confirmed that judgment. When asked to identify their activities over the last 30 days, born-again believers were just as likely to have gambled, visited pornographic websites, taken something that didn't belong to them, consulted a psychic, physically fought or abused someone, consumed enough alcohol to be legally drunk, used an illegal non-prescription drug, said something to someone that was not true, gotten back at someone for something he or she did, or said mean things behind another person's back.[60] Behaving this way as a follower of God is such a danger because He has called us to be light in this world.

> Don't frustrate God's work by showing up late, throwing a question mark over everything we're doing. Our work as God's servants gets validated—or not—in the details. People are watching us as we stay at our post, alertly, unswervingly . . . in hard times, tough times, bad times. (2 Corinthians 6:3–4 MSG)

Don't put a question mark over everything we are doing! Our work gets validated in the details. People are watching us. There is power in being a godly example, being light in a dark place. The government may try to silence your voice, but it cannot extinguish your light. There may be legislation, campus protocols, or workplace policies that will try to silence any mention of the name of Jesus, but none of them can steal the light of the gospel.

It is the difference between light versus lightning.

Let me explain what I mean. Lightning in the sky brings the "oohs" and "ahhs." It is the firework show. It captures people's attention for a moment. Light, on the other hand, is boring. It goes unnoticed, though it is desperately needed. If you are sitting in a room right now, you probably didn't take particular notice of the lights when you walked in. They sit there boringly. However, you sure would notice if they weren't there.

The lightning is the show. It might be a church service, a one-time street rally, a crusade. Lightning can happen on a Sunday, but light is every other moment of every day. Light may not be exciting, but it is essential. However, we seem to have this LED mentality, assuming that everything has to be big and explosive.

As believers, we are called to be light. Light is showing the fruit of the Spirit instead of the attitude of the age. It is demonstrating patience with the angry and the selfish, love to the marginalized, and peace to those who hate. Being light is when we maintain joy in hard times, practice gentleness in the midst of differing opinions, and choose meekness when others would show their power and title. You are light when you are kind to those of opposing or militant lifestyles, when your faithfulness goes unnoticed, and when you exercise self-control even though someone is provoking you.

One of the things I have learned over the years about evangelism is that they are right to call it the long game. Many times, I have seen people get saved through a conversation. However, I have noticed even more effective witnessing when things move from conversation to demonstration. People look at your life and wonder why you do things the way you do. Why do you live this way? How come you don't say things that way? It opens up the heart and mind.

The Bible exhorts us numerous times to be the light. It means that we are to be an example.

> For so the Lord commanded us, saying, "I have made you a light for the Gentiles, that you may bring salvation to the ends of the earth." (Acts 13:47 ESV)
>
> For at one time you were darkness, but now you are light

> in the Lord. Walk as children of light. (Ephesians 5:8 ESV)
>
> For you are all children of light, children of the day. We are not of the night or of the darkness. (1 Thessalonians 5:5 ESV)
>
> The night is far gone; the day is at hand. So then let us cast off the works of darkness and put on the armor of light. (Romans 13:12 ESV)
>
> That you may be blameless and innocent, children of God without blemish in the midst of a crooked and twisted generation, among whom you shine as lights in the world, holding fast to the word of life, so that in the day of Christ I may be proud that I did not run in vain or labor in vain. (Philippians 2:15–16 ESV)

Some time ago, I was walking with a non-Christian to a Middle Eastern restaurant, listening as he shared his opinions about Muslims. His comments were incredibly antagonistic, but I just listened as he went on a whole barrage of harsh words against Muslims. When he was finished, I told him about the testimonies of God's power in people's lives. As we entered the restaurant, we saw many people from Yemen who were there as servers and cashiers. All I wanted to do was be light to them, as well as to this man who was with me. So I showed love to these amazing people from Yemen, and I even invited them to church.

A look of amazement came over the man's face. He looked at me and said, "I've never seen anything like this." He was stunned because he had never seen an example. Everything with him was talk. An example is what begins to challenge people—not words but living out the fruit of the Spirit.

The Apostle Peter wrote to Christians who spent practically their whole lives walking with people who were not believers. The Christians he addressed were vastly outnumbered, and Peter wanted to teach them that when there are no words, their example is powerful.

> Friends, this world is not your home, so don't make yourselves cozy in it. Don't indulge your ego at the expense of your soul. Live an exemplary life among the people so that your actions will refute their prejudices. Then they'll be won over to God's side and be there to join in the celebration when he arrives. Make the Master proud of you by being good citizens. Respect the authorities, whatever their level; they are God's emissaries for keeping order. It is God's will that by doing good, you might cure the ignorance of the fools who think you're a danger to society. Exercise your freedom by serving God, not by breaking the rules. Treat everyone you meet with dignity. Love your spiritual family. Revere God. Respect the government. (1 Peter 2:11–17 MSG)

Peter is emphasizing being light through actions over mere words. He is challenging all of us to show Christ's love through our behavior. It can be as practical as saying "thank you" when you get your coffee or asking people, "How is your day going?" If you want to be light, take time to smile at people. Do small things. Hold a door open; pick up a piece of trash. Wave a car ahead of you. Tell people, "Have a great day" or say, "God bless you." Over time, something begins to happen.

After speaking about the power of a godly example, Peter then pivots to something you wouldn't expect. He goes right to Christ on the cross:

> For what credit is there if, when you sin and are harshly

> treated, you endure it with patience? But if when you do what is right and suffer for it you patiently endure it, this finds favor with God. For you have been called for this purpose, since Christ also suffered for you, leaving you an example for you to follow in His steps, who committed no sin, nor was any deceit found in His mouth; and while being reviled, He did not revile in return; while suffering, He uttered no threats, but kept entrusting Himself to Him who judges righteously; and He Himself bore our sins in His body on the cross, so that we might die to sin and live to righteousness; for by His wounds you were healed. For you were continually straying like sheep, but now you have returned to the Shepherd and Guardian of your souls. (1 Peter 2:20–25 NASB)

When speaking about representing Christ in the midst of unbelievers, Peter points to Jesus on the cross as our example. He then gives these instructions to all the wives:

> In the same way, you wives, be submissive to your own husbands so that even if any of them are disobedient to the word, they may be won without a word by the behavior of their wives, as they observe your chaste and respectful behavior. (1 Peter 3:1–2 NASB)

Some people get so worked up over the word "submissive" that they miss the whole point of the verses—"as they observe your chaste and respectful behavior." When you read 1 Peter 2:20–25 and consider all that Christ endured, it is mind-boggling. But what you don't realize is that you are being set up. This is what Peter does: He has you read about Christ's response to the sinful behavior of the authorities of His time, leaving you appalled and astounded. He sucks you into what Christ has done on the cross. And then out of nowhere, Peter hits you with four sledgehammer words: "In the same way."

The same way as what? The same way as Christ behaved. Peter is pointing us back to what Jesus has done, reminding us of the powerful example of the crucified Christ. He is highlighting the evangelistic power of godly behavior. A compelling witness can come from a life well-lived, even when your mouth is closed.

I believe this portion of Scripture is not just for wives trying to win unsaved husbands. There are principles here that can reach family members, coworkers, classmates, and other people in your life. Many can be won to Christ without a word but by your behavior.

Peter then goes into specifics:

> Your adornment must not be merely external—braiding the hair, and wearing gold jewelry, or putting on dresses; but let it be the hidden person of the heart, with the imperishable quality of a gentle and quiet spirit, which is precious in the sight of God. For in this way in former times the holy women also, who hoped in God, used to adorn themselves, being submissive to their own husbands; just as Sarah obeyed Abraham, calling him lord, and you have become her children if you do what is right without being frightened by any fear. (1 Peter 3:3–6 NASB)

In other words, spend more time working on the inside than anything else. It is the evangelistic power of a godly life—not with words but a lifestyle. The behavior of those who are believers in the home is key to salvation in the home.

Interestingly, this powerful principle goes back a decade before Peter's letter. Peter wrote his epistle in 64 AD. Ten years earlier, in 54 AD, Paul was addressing questions raised by the new church converts in Corinth. One of those questions is revealed through

Paul's answer in chapter 7. At that time, women were getting saved quicker than the men, so the women were asking this question: "If I'm saved now but my husband is not saved, can I divorce him?" Here was Paul's answer:

> But to the rest I say, not the Lord, that if any brother has a wife who is an unbeliever, and she consents to live with him, he must not divorce her. And a woman who has an unbelieving husband, and he consents to live with her, she must not send her husband away. For the unbelieving husband is sanctified through his wife, and the unbelieving wife is sanctified through her believing husband; for otherwise your children are unclean, but now they are holy. (1 Corinthians 7:12–14 NASB)

Paul was saying that the godly example in the home is stronger than the ungodly example. So when people object, "I don't want him influencing my kid," remember that the power of a godly life is what can permeate the home.

Ten years later, Peter dovetails on what Paul said and begins to show wives how to do it. Paul's message was, "Stay there." Then Peter adds, "In the same way, you will win them without a word by your behavior." Many of us have used words to try to lead people to Christ. But after a while, words stop working. People have heard it all: "Why aren't you a Christian yet?" "Are you finally coming to church?" Peter was saying that the only thing that will work now, the greatest weapon you have, is a godly lifestyle. We are supposed to be as Christ was on the cross:

> And while being reviled, He did not revile in return; while suffering, He uttered no threats, but kept entrusting Himself to Him who judges righteously. (1 Peter 2:23 NASB)

Let's look at the three things Peter mentions in this verse:

NO RETALIATIONS:

"While being reviled He did not revile . . ."

Just because a spouse does something to you, you are not to act in the same manner. They may argue, hit, mock, bring up the past, but you must not retaliate. We believe in turning the other cheek, not tit-for-tat. Why not remain silent and allow your light to shine as they are yelling at you? I have seen people on power trips simply because they are behind a counter, whether at a store or a TSA checkpoint, and everything in me starts rising up. It is in those moments that we must remind ourselves to be quiet, listen, smile, and show Christ.

NO THREATS:

"He uttered no threats . . ."

I believe Peter was saying to the wives that there should be no threats to leave or to divorce their spouse. That would be taking man's way out rather than God's. Instead, we are to say, "I am going to trust you, Lord."

TURN YOURSELF OVER TO THE FATHER:

". . . but kept entrusting Himself to Him who judges righteously."

Don't give up but give them up to God, and entrust yourself to the Father. The word "entrust" is the same word that was used for "betrayal" in the context of what Judas did to Jesus. It means "to hand over." You are betraying the flesh that loved to operate. You are handing it over, just as

> Judas handed over Jesus. You are handing your attitudes to the Father, and you are handing over the difficult person to Him as well.

We follow Christ's example when we refuse to retaliate or threaten others. Instead, we choose to continually give ourselves over to God. And remember, you are never more like Christ than when you choose forgive. On the cross, Jesus prayed to the Father to forgive those who crucified Him.

What else happened on the cross? We are amazed as Jesus brings a thief on the cross into paradise with Him. But there is someone else we often forget about: the soldier at the bottom of the cross.

> When the Roman military officer who was standing right in front of Jesus saw how he died, he said, "There is no doubt this man was the Son of God!" (Mark 15:39 TPT)

Jesus was not teaching or preaching when He was on the cross. But people saw the way He died. No threats, no retaliations, and He entrusted Himself to the Father. He was a light to the people who were underneath Him.

In the book of Psalms, there is an interesting verse about sowing. When we think of the biblical principle of sowing, the words "sowing" and "seeds" always go together. People often talk about sowing money, but the psalmist talks about sowing light.

> Light is sown like seed for the righteous. (Psalm 97:11 NASB)

Jesus tells us how this works—how we can be a light in the darkness. It is the only time I have seen in the Scriptures that we are called the same thing Jesus calls Himself. Jesus said in John 8:12, "I am the Light of the world." And in Matthew 5:14, He says to us, "You are the light of the world." How exactly does that work?

When I was growing up, I remember always going to VBS. We had to memorize verses, and we would get prizes for each verse we recited. One time I was so angry about the prize I received. I wanted a chocolate bar, but instead I got a glow-in-the-dark cross. I took that white cross out of my pocket and was even more upset when it didn't work. They gave me a bogus cross that didn't even glow in the dark. But then I finally flipped it over and read the instructions: Expose it to light, then it will glow in the dark.

I started to realize it is that simple. Every time I pray, I am exposing myself to the light. Every time I read the Word, light is coming. When you walk into a situation where the lights have been turned off, perhaps on your campus or at your job, you have an opportunity to glow in the dark. However, you have to expose yourself to the light first. A Christian who has not been exposed to the light does not glow in the dark. Instead, they become like what is out there.

Remember, we don't need to be lightning. It is not about being exciting; it is about being consistent. We are to be light in everything we do. It is having a smile, a godly attitude, the fruit of the Spirit. Show kindness and gratitude. Hold the door open for someone. Leave a good tip for your meal. That is how we glow in the dark. People may try to silence your voice, pointing to the manual that says you cannot talk about Jesus. But even if they silence your voice, they cannot stop your light.

In the book of Daniel, it is interesting to look at the three major protests he and his friends made in response to the darkness of the society they lived in. They took a stand regarding the king's diet, a 90-foot golden idol, and the no-prayer edict.

For the first one, Daniel was a negotiator. Instead of defiantly refusing to eat the king's food, Daniel respectfully asked, "Can we just eat our Jewish diet and then you can examine us ten days later?"

It was negotiated in kindness. The porter agreed, and the Bible says they looked ten times healthier and stronger than everybody else. Imagine if Daniel had stubbornly declared, "We won't eat." Daniel would have been a very short book. It probably would have read: "And they died bravely."

On the other hand, when it came to the 90-foot idol, there was no negotiation. Daniel's friends simply refused to bow, even if it meant being thrown into the fiery furnace. They stood firm because they had to obey the Scriptures.

Then when an edict was issued that no one could pray, Daniel just kept doing what he had already been doing. He was a man of prayer. When he was thrown into the lions' den, he was simply being light.

That is the challenge for us today: Be light. Sow light everywhere you go, every single day. When we are dealing with things like dietary restrictions or what we might call "gray areas," then we need God's grace. Not everything is a 90-foot idol that we must not bow to. I would say that about 10% of the issues we face will be the non-negotiable, "We ought to obey God rather than men" situations. When the Scriptures clearly tell us we must not bow, ask God for the courage of Daniel. But it won't be every issue. I believe the other 90% of what you will encounter will simply call for the fruit of the Spirit. That's when you must pray for the right attitude. Ask God to give you kindness, patience, and self-control. That is how you will shine, and Jesus reminds us what happens when people see our light:

> Let your light so shine before men, that they may see your good works and glorify your Father in heaven. (Matthew 5:16 NKJV)

We don't need exciting Christians. We just need consistent believers who will win others without a word by their behavior. Godly behavior is often a lot harder than words. It is easy to say, "Come to church with me." It is a whole other thing to live for Jesus and display the fruit of the Spirit. But that is how we shine, and our light will point people to God.

16

REDEFINING VERY GOOD (GENESIS 2 MEANS ROUND 2 OF THE BIG FIGHT)

We have arrived at not only the final chapter but also the most critical and the most controversial one. If we are going to win a billion souls, we must understand that we are in the midst of a fight. It is a fight that takes us back to the very beginning: Genesis chapter 1, the account of creation.

> God created man in His own image, in the image of God He created him; male and female He created them. God blessed them; and God said to them, "Be fruitful and multiply, and fill the earth, and subdue it; and rule over the fish of the sea and over the birds of the sky and over every living thing that moves on the earth." Then God said, "Behold, I have given you every plant yielding seed that is on the surface of all the earth, and every tree which has fruit yielding seed; it shall be food for you; and to every beast of the earth and to every bird of the sky and to every thing that moves on the earth which has life, I have given every green plant for food"; and it was so. God saw all that He had made, and behold, it was very good. (Genesis 1:27–31 NASB)

When God finished creating, He declared, "This is very good." However, people are now trying to redefine the "very good" of

Genesis 1. This is the battle we face. In fact, we are on round two of a fight that began about a hundred years ago.

I will begin with a rocky history, move to a tumultuous present, and then end with a vision for a glorious future. If you follow all the way to the end, you will understand why this message, though controversial, is critical for winning a billion souls. My goal is to equip you and to challenge this present culture with the truth of God's Word. So let's start by looking back at what took place in our nation over a century ago.

In 1925, a trial ignited a battle for our children's faith and the soul of every student in America, eventually spreading to different parts of the world. It seeped into almost all of the educational systems. Known as the Monkey Trial, it was officially titled The State of Tennessee v. John T. Scopes. This landmark legal battle centered on the teaching of evolution in public schools. Scopes was a high school teacher in Dayton, Tennessee. He was prosecuted for violating the Butler Act—a law that prohibited the teaching of evolution in public schools because it denied the biblical account of creation in Genesis. The trial became a media sensation, highlighting the growing clash between biblical Christianity and modern science. Scopes was found guilty. Although the trial did not overturn the Butler Act, it brought this issue of creation versus evolution into the national spotlight, sparking further debates.[61]

The battle continued for over six decades and has now settled into our schools—from elementary classrooms to universities—as well as in the sciences and government. The teaching of creationism as science was effectively banned in public schools by the U.S. Supreme Court in the 1987 landmark ruling of Edwards v. Aguillard.[62] Since then, we have seen creationism consistently attacked. Our children are indoctrinated in science classes with the teaching that it was a big bang instead of a big God that created it all. However, the battle was not just the fight between creationism and evolution. It was a fight to extinguish God from the minds of all people.

I grew up in a time when you would see things like a guy with multicolored hair holding up a sign in the endzone at a football game with the Scripture John 3:16. It was a verse that was appropriate for that era because people understood it. But over time, that verse has been removed from the minds and hearts of the public. What we need now is to hold up Genesis 1:1. We have to start from the beginning. We have to start with the fact that God does exist, that there was a beginning, and it was created by Him.

Man went after the existence of God and creationism a hundred years ago—the Genesis 1 battle. Now a Genesis 2 fight is in full battle mode. You weren't around in 1925 for the first battle, but you are present for this one.

It is in Genesis 2 that God created humanity.

> And He answered and said to them, "Have you not read that He who made them at the beginning made them male and female." Matthew 19:4 (NKJV)

God made them male and female. It was not the decision of man. But if you can remove God in Genesis 1, it makes it much easier to insert your laws over society.

When the world emerged after the COVID-19 pandemic, we awakened to "woke"—a vast number of people who are progressive regarding a number of social issues, especially when it comes to LGBTQ matters and gender identity. What once seemed to be a cultural battle was now considered normal, and those who oppose it are abnormal.

Just as Genesis 1 became banned by law and can no longer be taught to our children, the same is about to happen with Genesis 2. We are dealing with issues that Genesis 2 addresses: gender identity and same-sex marriage. Man is trying to create not only a new beginning of the universe but also a new beginning for people's birth—a new deciding factor for gender. Genesis 2 is also where God speaks of the sacredness of marriage, which Jesus affirmed in Matthew 19.

> Because God created this organic union of the two sexes, no one should desecrate his art by cutting them apart. They shot back in rebuttal. (Matthew 19:6–7 MSG)

Society is shooting back in rebuttal at what Genesis has to say about the beginning.

In short, here are the attacks:

Genesis 1 attack: There is no God, so I decide the foundational story. I decide where it all began. I decide from a classroom. If you remove God, then man decides what the story is with no empirical evidence.

Genesis 2 attack: There is no gender, so I decide who I am. It was said on Facebook that there are now 59 different genders you can choose from.

Genesis 3 attack: There is no sin. I decide what truth is.

It is a battle of the beginning—an attack on Genesis chapters 1, 2 and 3. God created the heavens and the earth; God made male and female. God created; God made. That's the common denominator: God was in charge. To merely call these things an allegory or myth is to begin to remove any type of accountability. If there is no God, then there is no truth. And if there is no truth, then there is no sin. If there is no sin, then there is no hell, which is a penalty. The removal of God is the removal of truth and responsibility. In essence, our society is saying, "I am God." We believe that we are sovereign and can decide what truth is.

Our society is attempting to redefine what God declared as "very good" at the end of Genesis 1 when He looked upon His creation. The Hebrew word "tov" for "good" implies order and proper function. But "very good" amplifies this to encompass the totality of creation, including humanity. It emphasizes the perfection and harmonious completeness of all of God's creation. It is not just a simple evaluation of good but a strong affirmation that everything is functioning as it should. Everything is fit together in a complete and beautiful way and does not need man's editing or touchup work.

Now the church finds itself at a crossroads. The Bible clearly tells us that from the beginning, marriage between a man and a woman has been a top priority for God. However, Christians today are caving in and accepting society's new definitions because they don't want to lose friends. Churches are caving in because they don't want to lose finances. What we desperately need in this hour are those who will stand for truth and speak boldly like the prophet Jeremiah.

It was a dark time for Israel in the days of Jeremiah. God was forsaken and the nation was backslidden. As a result, the enemy was at the door. The Lord called Jeremiah to begin prophesying and writing to His people in the kingdom of Judah. Jeremiah's cry during this crucial period was, "We must come back to God!"

> From Dan is heard the snorting of his horses; at the sound of the neighing of his stallions the whole land quakes; for they come and devour the land and its fullness, the city and its inhabitants. (Jeremiah 8:16 NASB)

They weren't in captivity yet, but Babylon was starting to close in on them. In the same way, today I hear the sound in the distance—the horses are coming. The snorting is not far away, and we must be a church that heeds God's warnings and helps lead our nation back to Him.

Before the enemy came in, Jeremiah asked four critical questions of his nation. He didn't ask "what"; he asked "why" questions. "What is happening?" identifies what the problem is. "Why is this happening?" goes to the root of the problem. It is a question that addresses the condition. "Why" says, "Enough of the band-aids. We need to demolish and renovate. We need to obey God!"

Jeremiah saw his nation in disrepair and in need of revival. We can look around and conclude the same thing about our nation. The four questions he asked Israel should be asked of all of us today.

WHY #1: WHY HAS THIS PEOPLE BACKSLIDDEN?

> Why has this people slidden back, Jerusalem, in a perpetual backsliding? They hold fast to deceit, they refuse to return. I listened and heard, but they do not speak aright. No man repented of his wickedness, saying, 'What have I done?' Everyone turned to his own course. (Jeremiah 8:5–6 NKJV)

They had abandoned God's Word and followed their own laws, just as we are doing today. We are placing critical decisions in the hands of broken people instead of in the hands of a God who is true and loving. Now we find ourselves in the midst of a battle. For example, there is currently a law in New York City that requires people to use whatever pronoun someone requests or be fined.

> How can you say, "We are wise, for we have the law of the Lord," when actually the lying pen of the scribes has handled it falsely? The wise will be put to shame; they will be dismayed and trapped. Since they have rejected the word of the Lord, what kind of wisdom do they have? (Jeremiah 8:8–9 NIV)

They made up their own laws, and this was the result:

> They heal the brokenness of the daughter of My people superficially, saying, "Peace, peace," but there is no peace. (Jeremiah 8:11 NASB)

No one was truly healed; nobody had peace. If you want peace today, it is found in one person: the Prince of Peace. There is nothing else that can bring peace to the soul or peace of mind other than Jesus Himself.

WHY #2: WHY ARE WE SITTING HERE?

> Why are we sitting here? (Jeremiah 8:14 NIV)

Much of the church today is afraid to move. We are afraid of backlash and persecution. We are aware that when you choose to stand for truth, you will be opposed. However, I have learned that the heat often gets turned up before Jesus shows up. It's the lesson of Daniel 3: what happens when you take a stand—just like the three Hebrew boys who refused to bow to the laws of Babylon. Jesus didn't show up in their defiance, He showed up in their fire. Taking a stand will draw attacks, but heaven will stand with you in the furnace.

WHY #3: WHY HAVE THEY PROVOKED ME?

> Why have they provoked Me? (Jeremiah 8:19 NKJV)

In the beginning of chapter 8, the Lord speaks through Jeremiah about how these people will come and dedicate godly things to the sun, the moon, and the host of heaven, which they also worshipped.

In a similar way, America didn't abandon God. We have simply added Him to everyone else's god. They call it pluralism. It tolerates Christianity, but it doesn't let Jesus become exclusively the way, the truth, and the life. Christianity simply becomes someone else's personal truth. We have provoked the true and living God to anger because we have allowed other gods to share His glory—yet the Lord has made it clear: He will not share His glory with another.

There is a structure in Rome called the Pantheon. When the ancient Romans conquered a nation, they would bring home that nation's gods and set a place in their temple for them. But when Christians were brought to Rome, there was no place for Jesus in the Pantheon. The followers of Jesus refused to give them an idol to put next to all the other gods. They would not treat Jesus like any other deity, and as a result, many of them were killed. They knew that the King of kings has no rival.

WHY #4 WHY HAS THEIR HEALTH NOT BEEN RESTORED?

> Why then has not the health of the daughter of my people been restored? (Jeremiah 8:22 NASB)

God challenged the spiritual leaders a few chapters later:

> The Lord replied: "Stop this foolishness and talk some sense! Only if you return to trusting me will I let you continue as my spokesman. You are to influence them, not let them influence you! They will fight against you like a besieging army against a high city wall. But they will not conquer you, for I am with you to protect and deliver you, says the Lord. Yes, I will certainly deliver you from these wicked men and rescue you from their ruthless hands." (Jeremiah 15:19–21 TLB)

We must speak truth. Leaders must take a stand. As believers, we are called to influence the world, not the other way around. Remember, the battle of Genesis 1 is to remove God. With no God, the battle of Genesis 2 is to make you god so you can define who you are. However, our true identity can only be found in God.

In essence, the Genesis 2 fight is over identity fraud. Identity fraud is when an unauthorized person gains access to your private assets. It is said that children, minors, college students, and young adults are the most susceptible to identity fraud.

Identity fraud doesn't just take place financially but spiritually as well. An unauthorized devil comes in and starts attacking minds. He whispers, "I know you were born that way, but this is what you really are." Ultimately, the enemy tries to get people to believe they have the right to redefine what is "very good."

You and I must fight for men and women, young and old, to have their true identity restored. Laws, emotions, and societal trends should not be allowed to define people who have been created in the image of God.

There is a fascinating story about orphans during World War II. After the bombing raids, thousands of children lost their families and became homeless. Some of the orphans were rescued and placed in refugee camps where they received food and care. However, they found that many of these children could not sleep at night because they were afraid of what tomorrow would bring. Would they wake up and find themselves homeless again? Would they have food? Nothing seemed to comfort them.

One day someone had the idea of giving each child a piece of bread to hold at bedtime. Holding their bread, these children were finally able to sleep in peace. All through the night, the bread reminded them, "Today, I ate, and I will eat again tomorrow."

I keep wondering what we have put our children and our society through. We have taken away the hope of tomorrow and have allowed questions to indoctrinate their minds. All of us need bread—the Bread of Life—every single day in order to live. Jesus said, "Give us this day our daily bread" (see Matthew 6:11). When you are starving, you will look for food anywhere and end up eating anything. That is why we must point people to the true Bread of Life.

> Jesus said to them, "I am the bread of life; he who comes to Me will not hunger, and he who believes in Me." (John 6:35 NASB)

You and I must help restore people's identity in Christ. One way is to let them know what God thinks about them. They must understand that their identity is not from themselves, from a government, or from a book. Our true identity is found in what God says about us in His Word. Whether you are speaking to Muslims, Jews, agnostics, atheists, or even believers who need to be reminded, here are some Scriptures that tell us how God feels about every single person:

1. HE MADE US IN HIS IMAGE

Then God said, "Let us make human beings in our image, to be like us." (Genesis 1:26 NLT)

2. YOU ARE GOD'S MASTERPIECE, HIS HANDIWORK

For we are God's masterpiece. He has created us anew in Christ Jesus, so we can do the good things he planned for us long ago. (Ephesians 2:10 NLT)

3. HE CROWNED YOU WITH GLORY AND HONOR

When I look at the night sky and see the work of your fingers—the moon and the stars you set in place—what are mere mortals that you should think about them, human beings that you should care for them? Yet you made them only a little lower than God and crowned them with glory and honor. (Psalm 8:3–5 NLT)

4. HE ORDAINED YOUR DAYS AND THINKS INNUMERABLE PRECIOUS THOUGHTS ABOUT YOU

Your eyes saw my unformed body; all the days ordained for me were written in your book before one of them came to be. How precious to me are your thoughts, God! How vast is the sum of them! Were I to count them, they would outnumber the grains of sand. (Psalm 139:16–18 (NIV)

5. HE WILL NEVER REJECT YOU

Whoever comes to me I will never drive away. (John 6:37 NIV)

6. HE DOESN'T WANT ANYONE TO PERISH

He is not willing that any should perish, and he is giving more time for sinners to repent. (2 Peter 3:9 TLB)

7. HE LOVES THIS WORLD

For God so loved the world that He gave His only begotten Son, that whoever believes in Him should not perish but have everlasting life. (John 3:16 NKJV)

8. HE LOVED US SO MUCH THAT HE SENT HIS SON TO DIE FOR US

But God demonstrates His own love toward us, in that while we were still sinners, Christ died for us. (Romans 5:8 NKJV)

9. HE CAN MAKE YOU INTO A NEW PERSON, REGARDLESS OF YOUR PAST

Therefore, if anyone is in Christ, he is a new creation; old things have passed away; behold, all things have become new. (2 Corinthians 5:17 NKJV)

10. HE LONGS TO FORGIVE YOU

But if we freely admit our sins when his light uncovers them, he will be faithful to forgive us every time. God is just to forgive us our sins because of Christ, and he will continue to cleanse us from all unrighteousness. (1 John 1:9 TPT)

11. HE ACCEPTS YOU RIGHT NOW

Therefore, accept each other just as Christ has accepted you so that God will be given glory. (Romans 15:7 NLT)

12. HE NEVER STOPS KNOCKING ON THE DOOR OF YOUR HEART

Behold, I'm standing at the door, knocking. If your heart is open to hear my voice and you open the door within, I will come in to you and feast with you, and you will feast with me. (Revelation 3:20 TPT)

Our minds are constantly under assault because the heart is such a valuable spot that the enemy targets. If he can get your mind thinking a certain way, you will succumb to it. This goes beyond issues of gender. The enemy is trying to define who people are at the core. It is not just unbelievers who have to fight lies; many believers also face doubts about their identity in Christ. Many people don't go to sleep at night with bread.

Allow me to give you some bread to hold onto and have ready to share with others. Here are 30 slices of bread from the Scriptures:

You are accepted. (Romans 15:7)
You are chosen. (John 15:16)
You are free. (Galatians 4:7)
You are forgiven. (1 John 1:9)
You are a new person. (2 Corinthians 5:17)
You are a child of God. (John 1:12)
You are made in God's image. (Genesis 1:27)
You belong to Jesus. (1 Corinthians 3:23)
You have been given new life. (Romans 6:4)
You are a citizen of heaven. (Philippians 3:20)
You are protected by God. (1 Peter 1:5)
You are part of what God is doing. (1 Corinthians 12:27)
God loves you no matter what. (Romans 8:38–39)
God is with you. (Zephaniah 3:17)
You are seen specifically. (Psalm 139:13–16)
You are precious to God. (Isaiah 43:4)
You have been rescued. (Galatians 3:13)
God has a plan for your life. (Jeremiah 29:11)
God listens to you. (1 John 5:14–15)
God gives you strength. (Philippians 4:13)
You are an heir. (Romans 8:17)

You are part of God's family. (Ephesians 2:19)
The Holy Spirit lives in you. (1 Corinthians 6:19)
God is taking care of you. (Psalm 23:1–3)
Jesus gives you true joy. (John 15:11)
You are blessed. (Ephesians 1:3)
Jesus gave himself for you. (Galatians 2:20)
God understands you. (Psalm 139:1)
You are treasured by God. (Exodus 19:5)
You are complete in Christ. (Colossians 2:10)

Cindy and I needed that bread when we first got married and lived in a dangerous area of Detroit. My associate pastor lived one block over from us. One day, someone broke into his house and stabbed him 38 times. Miraculously, he survived. To this day, he has six to eight feet of scarring on his body to remind him that God is a miracle worker. You can be sure he needed 30 slices of bread every moment of his walk after that tragedy.

The day came when he was sitting in court, facing the man who had stabbed him 38 times. When asked to give a victim statement. He said, "Absolutely not. I'll give a victor statement." And he did. I watched as he began to read those 30 slices of bread. God is using him now to minister to prisoners on death row. He is walking murderers to Christ, showing them the way to salvation![63]

We lived three houses apart. It could have happened at our house. I wasn't even there at the time, so it could have been Cindy and the four kids. After the incident, Cindy was having dreams every night that someone was breaking into our house and killing all of us. We began praying and declaring, "I bind you, Satan!" But one day we found a slice of bread in Proverbs 6:

> My son, observe the commandment of your father and do not forsake the teaching of your mother; bind them

> continually on your heart; tie them around your neck. (Proverbs 6:20–21 NASB)

Instead of binding the enemy, we started binding the Word on our hearts. Every single night, we would read the Scriptures over our lives. We would take a slice of bread whenever the enemy whispered, "You're not going to wake up tomorrow. I'm sending murderers." Here is the good news. Look at what happens when you bind the Word on your heart:

> When you walk about, they will guide you; when you sleep, they will watch over you; and when you awake, they will talk to you. (Proverbs 6:22 NASB)

That Word became like a canopy over us, and suddenly it was as if the enemy's missiles couldn't break through. As we read the Scriptures, I would say, "God, this is Your Word. It says that when I sleep, the Word will guard me. It will guard my mind." That is why the last thing to do at night is not check social media. Put the Word over your heart.

It is very important that you do not forget to eat your daily bread, and offer others the Bread of Life as well. Jesus promised that whoever comes to Him will never be hungry again (see John 6:25). We won't hunger for identity. We won't hunger for somebody or something else to define us and make us valuable. We are already valuable. We are made in the image of God.

Let's choose not to allow people, culture, laws, or governments to redefine what God has already declared as "very good." One billion truly does start with one. One identity restored, one life transformed by the gospel can be a catalyst for changing a dorm room, a college campus, a community, a nation, and even the world. And it all starts with one person willing to step out in faith: you.

NOTES

INTRODUCTION

1 James Hudson Taylor Quotes, Goodreads, accessed September 29, 2025, https://www.goodreads.com/quotes/799214-the-great-commission-is-not-an-option-to-be-considered.

2 Leonard Ravenhill, *Weeping Between the Porch and the Altar*, audio sermon, August 21, 2009 (originally delivered earlier), SermonAudio.com, accessed December 3, 2025, https://www.sermonaudio.com/zh/sermons/82109947506/a.

3 Charles H. Spurgeon, "She Was Not Hidden," in *The Metropolitan Tabernacle Pulpit*, vol. 34 (London: Passmore & Alabaster, 1888), 232.

4 Mother Teresa, *Mother Teresa: A Simple Path* (New York: Ballantine Books, 1995), 31.

CHAPTER 1

5 Brennan Manning, *The Ragamuffin Gospel: Good News for the Bedraggles, Beat-Up, and Burnt Out* (Colorado Springs, CO: Multnomah Books, 1990), 102.

6 C.S. Lewis, *Reflections on the Psalms* (San Diego: Harcourt Brace Jovanovich, 1958), 9.

7 Mother Teresa, *My Dear Children: Mother Teresa's Last Message*, ed. Hiroshi Katayanagi (New York: Paulist Press, 2001), 28-29

8 Brian L. Powell, "Duck Church," *Brian L Powell* (blog), October 30, 2015, https://brianlpowell.com/2015/10/30/duck-church/.

CHAPTER 2

9 P.P. Job, *Why, God, Why?* (Tortured for Christ Publications, 2000), 113-116.

10 Charles Grandison Finney Quotes, Goodreads, accessed September 27, 2025, https://www.goodreads.com/author/quotes/4645522.Charles_Grandison_Finney.

11 David Brainerd, *The Life and Diary of David Brainerd*, Jonathan Edwards, ed. (Edinburgh: The Banner of Truth Trust, 2002), 124.

12 Charles Haddon Spurgeon Quotes, Goodreads, accessed September 27, 2025, https://www.goodreads.com/quotes/8561226-the-word-of-god-is-like-a-

lion-you-don-t.

CHAPTER 3

13 "Lincoln Frees a Slave," *Preaching Today*, accessed November 18, 2025, https://www.preachingtoday.com/illustrations/2001/july/13140.html.

CHAPTER 4

14 James Hudson Taylor Quotes, Goodreads.

15 Leonard Ravenhill, *Why Revival Tarries 2nd ed.* (Chicago: Moody Press, 1983), #.

16 Rodney Stark, *The Rise of Christianity: How the Obscure, Marginal Jesus Movement Became the Dominant Religious Force in the Western World in a Few Centuries* (New York: Harper Collins, 1997), #.

17 For a full description of the Azusa Street Revival, see Sonny Arguinzoni Sr., *Treasures Out of Darkness* (La Puente, CA: Victory Outreach Pub., 1996).

18 Dwight L. Moody, *Secret Power*, or the Secret of Success in Christian Life and Work (Chicago: Fleming H. Revell, 1881), 28.

19 Joseph S. Batluck Sr., "Teen Challenge International: The Impact He Has Made Globally Is Immeasurable," *ACCOLADE* (Teen Challenge Internations, USA), July 2017, http://victoryoutreach.org/wp-content/uploads/2017/07/Joseph-Batluck-ACCOLADE.pdf](http://victoryoutreach.org/wp-content/uploads/2017/07/Joseph-Batluck-ACCOLADE.pdf.

CHAPTER 5

20 David Wilkerson, B*eyond the Cross and the Switchblade* (Grand Rapids, MI: Chosen Books, 1974), 35-37.

21 James Dobson, *Coming Home: Timeless Wisdom for Families* (Wheaton IL: Tyndale Publishing, 1999), 122.

22 *We Bought a Zoo*, directed by Cameron Crowe (Beverly Hills, CA: 20th Century Fox, 2011), Film.

23 Carmine Gallo, "How Steve Jobs and Bill Gates Inspired John Sculley to Pursue the 'Noble Cause,'" *Forbes*, November 12, 2016, https://www.forbes.com/sites/carminegallo/2016/11/12/how-steve-jobs-and-bill-gates-inspired-john-sculley-to-pursue-the-noble-cause/.

24 Michael Parrot, *Street Level Evangelism: Where Is the Space for the Local Evangelist?* (Spokane, WA: Acts Evangelism, 1993) 9-11.

25 While the exact wording of this quote differs across different sources, its sentiment is widely attributed to Billy Graham. See Billy Graham, as quoted in Bill Fay, *Share Jesus Without Fear* (Nashville: Broadman & Holman, 1999), 114.

CHAPTER 6

26 While this is not a direct quote from Aquinas's original writings, the phrasing is widely attributed to the following source: Sydney J. Harris, *Pieces of Eight: Being Arguments in Favor of Living a Decent Life* (New York: Harper & Row, 1982), 105.

27 See Rosaria Champagne Butterfield, *The Secret Thoughts of an Unlikely Convert: An English Professor's Journey into Christian Faith* (Pittsburgh: Crown & Covenant, 2012), Kindle.

28 National Institute of Mental Health, *Mental Illness*, Last modified January 2024, https://www.nimh.nih.gov/health/statistics/mental-illness.

29 *The Jesus Film*, https://give.cru.org/jesusfilmproject-priorities.html and https://www.baptistpress.com/resource-library/news/jesus-film-viewership-surpasses-5-billion/

30 Michael D. Lindsay, *Hinge Moments: Making the Most of Life's Transitions* (Downers Grove, IL: InterVarsity Press, 2021), ii-iv.

CHAPTER 7

31 "250 QUOTES BY LEONARD RAVENHILL" A-Z Quotes, accessed July 6, 2025, https://www.azquotes.com/author/38314-Leonard_Ravenhill?p=10.

32 The text is a summary of C.T. Studd's life, incorporating facts widely documented in numerous historical and biographical sources.

33 Leonard Sweet (@lensweet), "China is on track to have more Christians than the entire population of the United States . . . ." *X* (tweet), December 13, 2024, 9 p.m.

34 Although the article's exact title is debated, Jillian Kay Melchior's *Wall Street Journal* opinion piece, published on October 22, 2015, about evangelical adoption and the refugee crisis, includes this reference.

35 "Africa Population (Live)," *Worldometer*, accessed July 6, 2025. https://www.worldometers.info/world-population/africa-population/.

36 Todd M. Johnson and Gina A. Zurlo, eds. 2024, "Status of Global Christianity, 2024, in the *International Bulletin of Mission Research," International Bulleting of Mission Research* 48, no 1: 27-38.

CHAPTER 8

37 Thomas E. Bergler, *The Juvenilization of American Christianity* (Grand Rapids, MI: Wm. B. Eerdmans Publishing Co., 2012), 141-146.

38 Bergler, *Juvenilization*, 20-45.

39 Billy Graham, QuoteFancy, accessed September 30, 2025, https://

quotefancy.com/quote/775855/Billy-Graham-To-get-nations-back-on-their-feet-we-must-first-get-down-on-our-knees.

40 "Tozer: Pathways Into Revival," *Pray for Revival!* September 21, 2015, https://prayforrevival.wordpress.com/2015/09/20/tozer-pathways-into-revival/.

41 *Christians Together,* "The Hebrides Revival," accessed November 18, 2025, https://www.christianstogether.net/Articles/94936/Revival_in_the.aspx.

42 Johnny Oleksinski, "Andrew Lloyd Webber Dreams of Buying This Famous Theater: 'The Best Stage on Broadway,'" *New York Post*, May 12, 2025. https://nypost.com/2025/05/12/entertainment/andrew-lloyd-webber-dreams-of-buying-this-famous-theater-the-best-stage-on-broadway/.

CHAPTER 9

43 C.S. Lewis, *Mere Christianity* (New York: Macmillan Publishing Co, 1952), 171.

44 "Garbage Barge Mobro Cruises U.S. Atlantic and Gulf Coasts," *EBSCO Information Services, Inc.*, accessed September 30, 2025, https://www.ebsco.com/research-starters/history/garbage-barge-mobro-cruises-us-atlantic-and-gulf-coasts.

CHAPTER 10

45 Lee Strobel, *The Case for Faith: A Journalist Investigates the Toughest Objections to Christianity* (Grand Rapids, MI: Zondervan Publishing House, 2000), 13-14.

CHAPTER 11

46 See UL Research Institutes' Fire Safety Research Institute (FSRI), *Southern California Fires Timeline Report* (November 2025), https://fsri.org/research-update/southern-california-fires-timeline-report.

47 "Interagency Hotshot Crews," *U.S. Department of Agriculture: Forest Service*, accessed July 13, 2025, https://www.fs.usda.gov/science-technology/fire/people/hotshots.

48 Hillsong Worship, "Stronger," on *This Is Our God*, words and music by Ben Fielding and Reuben Morgan (Hillsong Music Australia, 2008), compact disc. Used by permission.

CHAPTER 13

49 The quote is widely attributed to D. L. Moody and appears in numerous collections of anecdotes and Christian literature, though its precise original source (a specific sermon transcript or publication date) is a matter of debate. The story is generally presented as an anecdote about Moody's evangelistic approach and dedication to ensuring that everyone heard the gospel message.

50 Shannon L. Alder Quotes, Goodreads, accessed August 16, 2025, https://

www.goodreads.com/author/quotes/1391130.Shannon_L_Alder?page=15.

51 Leonard Ravenhill, QuoteFancy, accessed October 2, 2025, https://quotefancy.com/quote/852335/Leonard-Ravenhill-Jesus-did-not-come-into-the-world-to-make-bad-men-good-He-came-into-the.

CHAPTER 14

52 Ferdinand Funk, "The Story Is Told That After Helen Kellers," SermonCentral, September 26, 2008, https://www.sermoncentral.com/sermon-illustrations/69045/the-story-is-told-that-after-helen-keller-s-by-ferdinand-funk.

53 C.S. Lewis, *The Weight of Glory* (New York: Harper Collins, 2001), 46.

54 C.S. Lewis, *A Grief Observed* (New York: Harper Collins, 2001) 22-23.

55 C. S. Lewis, *Mere Christianity* (New York: Harper Collins, 2001), 136-137.

56 See https://www.facebook.com/watch/?v=1432258981416492 Praise on TBN

CHAPTER 15

57 Bobby Conway, "The Fifth Gospel: The Ultimate Apologetic," *Christian Research Institute*, updated April 12, 2023, https://www.equip.org/articles/fifth-gospel-ultimate-apologetic/.

58 Charles Haddon Spurgeon, *"The Clean and the Unclean"* 1863, The Spurgeon Center, accessed August 26, 2025. https://www.spurgeon.org/ resource-library/sermons/the-clean-and-the-unclean/#flipbook/.

59 David Kinnaman and Gabe Lyons, *unChristian: What a New Generation Really Thinks About Christianity . . . and Why It Matters* (Grand Rapids, MI: Baker Books, 2007), 54.

60 George Barna, *Boiling Point: Answering the Critics Who Denounce Born-Again Christianity* (Ventura, CA: Regal Books, 1998), 108–110.

CHAPTER 16

61 Mindy Johnston, *"Scopes Trial," Encyclopaedia Britannica*, last modified July 21, 2025, https://www.britannica.com/event/Scopes-Trial.

62 Vivian Hopp Gordon, "Edwards v. Aguillard," *Encyclopaedia Britannica*, last modified June 12, 2025, https://www.britannica.com/topic/Edwards-v-Aguilard.

63 Dennis Linn, Sheila Fabricant Linn, and Matthew Linn. *Sleeping with Bread: Holding What Gives You Life* (Mahwah, NJ: Paulist Press, 1995), 1.

ALSO AVAILABLE

FROM TIM DILENA

GET INSIGHT

Discover life-changing lessons from each New Testament chapter, one day at a time.

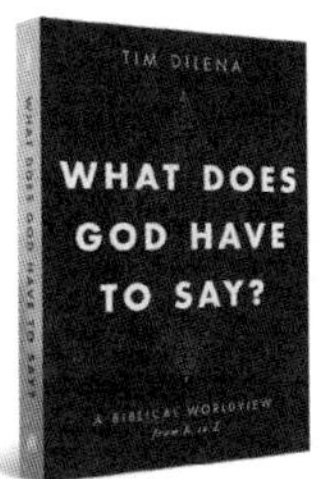

STAND FIRM

Learn God's principles to hold steady in an unstable world.

TRUST GOD

See how God can lead you through life's ups and downs.

LEARN TO PRAY

Discover 101 ways to talk to God about your struggles, like fear, forgiveness, anxiety and more.

DON'T GIVE UP

Nurture a daily mindset to keep you moving forward in life and in faith.

BREAK THROUGH

Experience how the power of prayer can change everything.

For more spiritual insight to help you thrive in everyday life:

Explore
messages and books at
tsc.nyc

Follow us

@TimesSquareChurch

@PastorTimDilena

TIMES SQUARE ▣ CHURCH

1657 Broadway NY, NY 10019
tsc.nyc